Praise for Healing Family Relationships

"All families are messy and, at times, broken. All families need healing. Rob Rienow writes with such authenticity and knowledge as to be a sort of spiritual mentor to help you find that healing with your family relationships. There is not a family in the universe who would not benefit from this book. It's hope filled, biblical, and practical."

—Jim Burns, PhD, president, HomeWord; author
of *Doing Life with Your Adult Children: Keep Your Mouth Shut
& the Welcome Mat Out* and *The Purity Code*

"Are you struggling to maintain strong, healthy bonds with your family members? We've all found ourselves at odds with loved ones from time to time, but Rob Rienow's latest book will show you how to experience healing in your most important relationships this side of heaven."

—Jim Daly, president, Focus on the Family

"Anything Rob Rienow writes is worth reading. In my opinion, no one is better at applying God's Word to the complexities of marriage and family and multigenerational faithfulness than Rob. Read *Healing Family Relationships* and be equipped and inspired and challenged to love God and family like never before."

—Troy Dobbs, senior pastor, Grace Church of Eden Prairie

"Have you reached a dead end in trying to heal broken relationships in your family? Rob Rienow will provide you with a whole host of new strategies that are biblical and practical. His personal transparency is exemplary, and his wisdom is biblical. This is simply the best book I've ever read on the topic!"

—Larry Fowler, founder, the Legacy Coalition

"Rob Rienow understands what it means, theologically and practically, to foster healing in family relationships. This book is a treasure trove for parents and grandparents hoping to cultivate healing, grace, and peace during seasons of familial brokenness, sin, and spiritual warfare."

—Dr. Brian Haynes, lead pastor,
Bay Area Church and Christian School

"Nobody is exempt from the hurts and wounds that come from being part of a family—even a loving family. They're inevitable. But not everyone rises above the pain to build better relationships. Why? It's tough. Thankfully, Rob Rienow has provided a biblically based path for doing just that in *Healing Family Relationships*. Don't miss out on this life-transforming message."

—Drs. Les & Leslie Parrott, #1 *New York Times* bestselling
authors of *Saving Your Marriage Before It Starts*

"Rob begins this remarkable book with the comforting assurance that messy families are normal. Then with transparency and wisdom, he offers a sensible, biblical blueprint for restoration, healing, and hope. No matter how dysfunctional your family might be, this book will help you strengthen relationships with the people you love most."

—Wayne Rice, cofounder of Youth Specialties,
conference director of the Legacy Coalition

"Minutes after reading *Healing Family Relationships*, I ordered copies to give to people I care about. And right after that, I made the book required reading in my seminary course on the family. I cannot give a stronger endorsement than those two actions. This is an *important* book."

—Richard Ross, PhD, professor of student ministry,
Southwestern Seminary, Fort Worth, Texas

"Only God can heal broken family relationships. In this very personal, touching book, Rob shows us how to position ourselves well while we wait for that healing. And if God chooses not to heal the relationship, this book opens pathways for God to heal us."

—Dr. Scott Turansky, cofounder,
National Center for Biblical Parenting

HEALING
Family
Relationships

HEALING
Family
Relationships

A Guide to Peace and Reconciliation

ROB RIENOW

BETHANYHOUSE

a division of Baker Publishing Group
Minneapolis, Minnesota

Published by Bethany House Publishers
11400 Hampshire Avenue South
Bloomington, Minnesota 55438
www.bethanyhouse.com

Bethany House Publishers is a division of
Baker Publishing Group, Grand Rapids, Michigan

Printed in the United States of America

Library of Congress Cataloging-in-Publication Data
Names: Rienow, Rob, author.
Title: Healing family relationships : a guide to peace and reconciliation / Rob Rienow.
Description: Minneapolis : Bethany House Publishers, 2020. | Summary: "Every family is hurting, and the wounds that come from our relatives can be deeper than all others. Offering powerful, actionable steps, Rob Rienow presents personal stories of various families and key biblical examples that will help readers pursue peace and healing in their home""—Provided by publisher.
Identifiers: LCCN 2019054282 | ISBN 9780764235306 (trade paperback) | ISBN 9781493424900 (ebook)
Subjects: LCSH: Families—Religious aspects—Christianity. | Families—Religious aspects.
Classification: LCC BT707.7 .R54 2020 | DDC 261.8/3585—dc23
LC record available at https://lccn.loc.gov/2019054282

Cover design by Darren Welch Design

20   21   22   23   24   25   26   7   6   5   4   3   2   1

To John Diehl,
my brother-in-law,
who is home in heaven with Jesus.
Thank you, John,
for being a person of peace.

Contents

Acknowledgments

A special thanks to my wife, Amy, most importantly for always seeking healing and reconciliation with me in and through our conflicts, but also for helping me improve every aspect of this book. Thanks also to my mother and stepfather, Angie and Jack, for their labor of love in proofreading. I am thankful that this book on family relationships has been a family project.

Introduction

Every Family Is Hurting

Every family experiences conflict, hurt, and brokenness. There are two big reasons for this reality. First, each of us struggles with sin and character problems. When multiple people with character problems live together under the same roof, you get lots of problems! Second, God created the family as the foundation of all human life and society. Satan and his demons understand this, so a tremendous amount of their firepower is directed toward breaking the relationships between spouses, parents and children, and brothers and sisters.

I believe you picked up this book because you desire healing in one of your family relationships—or perhaps for your entire family tree. There is good news! God loves your family. He intentionally put the members of your family together. He has the power to use the joys and the sorrows of your family's journey to draw you closer to Him and to one another. In the pages ahead you will not find pat answers or quick fixes. However, you will find encouragement, hope, and principles from the Bible that will give you practical steps toward healing broken relationships in your family and experiencing more peace in your home.

We need God's power every day in the Rienow home. Amy and I have been married since 1994, and we have been blessed with seven children. That adds up to nine sinful people living under the same roof! Let's run the math on that for a moment. There are thirty-six relationships in our house. I have a unique relationship with eight people—my wife and seven kids. My wife has a unique relationship with seven people, as her relationship with me is counted in my list. When you add it all up, there are thirty-six individual relationships. Do you know what that means? Not a single day goes by where we don't have problems, conflicts, and blowups of one kind or another. We are in daily need of mercy, grace, and forgiveness.

The struggles within our homes are compounded by challenging relationships with parents, in-laws, and extended family. Not only do we have the problems and hurts of today, but many families are feeling the consequences of past wounds and generational brokenness.

I was not born into what anyone would call a healthy family tree. My mother was my father's fourth wife. My father was my mother's second husband. Neither of them knew the Lord when I was born. When I was fifteen years old, my parents divorced due in large part to my father's infidelity. Even through all this sadness and brokenness, God's healing power has been at work. The Lord brought my mother, and later my father, to faith in Jesus. He has blessed Amy and me through all the joys and struggles of our marriage relationship and is now using us to raise the next generation to follow Him.

God is in the business of taking broken things and making them whole. He loves to bring joy out of ashes. It is not too late for my family, and it is not too late for yours. Through Christ we can be reconciled with God and reconciled with one another.

Reconciliation, however, is not a passive process. Many times, while we are struggling with family conflicts and dysfunction, we rightly *desire* for things to be better, and yet we are not taking intentional and *active steps* toward healing. It takes more than good intentions to seek healing in a relationship.

Be Patient

Healing is usually a slow process—especially healing from family wounds. This is not a book of magic formulas or quick fixes. The biblical principles here will give you guidance and encouragement for what may be a long journey. Some of the chapters may not fit your specific family situation, while others may contain the exact biblical principles you need to take a step toward reconciliation. The Lord will not abandon you as you take small steps toward healing.

If you are in an active situation of abuse, abandonment, adultery, addiction, or another major crisis, please call your pastor or local Christian counselor. While the biblical principles and stories[1] we will explore here are meant to provide hope and help to you, I would recommend reading this book alongside other resources specifically focused on those crisis situations.

Read with a Friend

God often uses friends to support us while we heal. Also, our friends can help us with needed objectivity regarding our family conflicts. Sometimes it takes someone from outside the family to offer us truth and clarity. Consider asking a friend, or your small group, to read along and pray with you through this process. Consider meeting periodically to share what God is teaching you and receive encouragement.

Prepare for Action

This book is packed with Scriptures of encouragement and hope, but also action. I pray that as you read, the Lord will strengthen you and enable you to put these biblical principles into practice so that your family, and the future generations that come from it, will be blessed, be filled with peace, overflow with love, and shine for Christ.

Chapter 1

The Power of Forgiveness

Therefore, if anyone is in Christ, he is a new creation. The old has passed away; behold, the new has come. All this is from God, who through Christ reconciled us to himself and gave us the ministry of reconciliation.

2 Corinthians 5:17–18

A happy, loving, peaceful home. Can you think of any earthly blessing greater than this? I want more happiness, love, and peace in my home. I believe God wants that too. Many people have told me they would trade all their money and success for loving relationships at home.

At the beginning of creation, God carefully and intentionally established the institution of the family. More recently, He carefully and intentionally created *your* family. He chose your parents for you. He chose your siblings for you. At this point, some of you are saying, "God, what were you thinking? I support your whole idea of the family, but the combination of people you put in my house just isn't working!"[1] The challenges in our families are not a surprise to God. He desires to use all those struggles and conflicts to draw us closer to Him, and to help us experience His gift of forgiveness and reconciliation.

The purpose of this first chapter is to establish some foundational points about the nature of forgiveness and reconcili-

> ## The challenges in our families are not a surprise to God.

ation. In the chapters that follow, we will explore personal and practical ways to pursue peace and healing in our family relationships.

The Crucible of Family Relationships

Your family is like a crucible. A crucible is a ceramic pot into which you put impure metal, and then under high heat the impurities separate from the metal and can be removed. Under the intense heat of family relationships our real character is revealed—the best and, far too often, the worst. Who we are at home is who we really are. Our true nature and character show up when we walk into our home and close the door. Why is it that I can easily go through a whole day at work without losing my patience with my co-workers, but then I lose my cool with the kids within ten minutes of arriving home? Because home life is real life.

Consider how great God's divine plan is. The intense heat of our family relationships draws out the things in our character that need to be sanctified. These ugly traits and behaviors come out at home with those whom God created to love us unconditionally and stick with us no matter what. Isn't that a great plan? Can you imagine if our temper, impatience, and selfishness regularly came out at work, school, or church? We would not last long at any of those places.

By God's design, the heat of family relationships brings everyone's character flaws to the surface. Put bluntly, family relationships reveal a lot of sin. This is part of God's plan that

> **If we desire greater happiness, peace, and love in our homes, we must become experts in giving and receiving forgiveness.**

we might grow in faith, character, and godliness. But none of this growth will happen without an essential ingredient— *forgiveness*. If we desire greater happiness, peace, and love in our homes, we must become experts in giving and receiving forgiveness.

Bitter Roots

In Hebrews 12:14–15, God tells us, *"Strive for peace with everyone, and for the holiness without which no one will see the Lord. See to it that no one fails to obtain the grace of God; that no 'root of bitterness' springs up and causes trouble, and by it many become defiled."*

The call here is to "strive for peace with everyone," and if we are to do that with our family members, we must "see to it . . . that no 'root of bitterness' springs up." God gives us a planting analogy for relationships and the effects of bitterness and unforgiveness. A family conflict starts with sin. It is a seed of offense and hurt. Sometimes, when we experience hurt and rejection from someone at home, we tell ourselves, "I'll just take the high road here and let it go. Time heals all wounds." While there can be value in choosing not to be easily provoked, it is simply not true that "time heals all wounds." If you got a deep gash in your arm, you would not look at the open flesh and say, "No problem. I'll just let that go. Time heals all wounds." With major wounds, time without treatment leads to infection and far worse.

In the same way, if you plant a seed and then walk away and forget about it, what is that seed going to do? It is going to grow roots, sprout into a plant, and eventually bear fruit. The same thing happens when a seed of hurt is planted in our hearts. Unless we specifically address it through an intentional forgiveness process, it will grow a "root of bitterness." Notice, then, that a root of bitterness always grows up to do two things. First, what grows from that root is going to cause trouble; and second, it will defile many. To *defile* means "to pollute or corrupt." We see that second ugly effect in our home on an ongoing basis. Two people get into a conflict, and before we know it, all nine of us are going at it! Bitter roots do indeed spring up to cause trouble and corrupt many. This is why it is so urgent that we deal with the seed and any roots before they produce their destructive fruit.

A few years ago, I was leading Visionary Family Conferences in Malaysia, and while I was there I learned Southeast Asia is home to one of the fastest-growing trees in the world. The batai tree grows so fast it has been called the miracle tree. When a seed is planted, a month may pass without any sign of life above the ground. In two months, the sprout may only be a foot high. However, the tree can grow more than twenty feet in the first season. From there it can reach as high as 120 feet.[2] They say you can hear it cracking as it grows. This type of tree grows very slowly in the early stages. The seed first sends out long, strong roots, gathering nutrients for its eventual burst upward.

A seed of hurt can work just like the seed from this plant. It goes in the ground, and although unseen, it immediately goes to work developing the tree's root system. Then a small sprout emerges, and before we know it we are confronted with a full-size tree. Some of our current family conflicts are the result of seeds of hurt, and roots of bitterness, that were planted long ago.

The Call to Forgive

One of the most powerful Scriptures on forgiveness is also one of the shortest. God says in Colossians 3:13, "*As the Lord has forgiven you, so you also must forgive.*" Here God compares His forgiveness of our sins to our forgiveness of others.

Think of a specific family member with whom you have had conflict. Let's apply this passage to that relationship. Imagine an old-fashioned scale, the type of scale that balances two platforms. Objects can be placed on opposite sides, and the scale will reveal which object is heavier.

While this may not be a pleasant exercise, I would ask you to think about this family member who has hurt you. Imagine a pile on one side of the scale of all the things the person has done to wound you. On the other side of the scale, imagine a pile of all the sins you have ever committed against God. Which side is heavier? To which side does the scale tip? The point here is not to minimize the wounds you have received from your family. For some of us, those wounds are serious and grievous. However, the sins committed against us are greatly outweighed by the sins we have committed against God. In this simple verse in Colossians, God directs our attention to His extraordinary forgiveness of our sins, which He made possible through the death of His Son, and then He calls us to follow His example and forgive those who have sinned against us.

21

Forgiving My Father

My greatest struggle in family forgiveness was with my father. Our story will be woven through the pages ahead. In the introduction, I shared with you that my father's infidelity led to my parents' divorce. As a fifteen-year-old, I was bitter and angry at what he had done to Mom and how his bad behavior had separated our family. At the time, I had some well-meaning Christian friends who encouraged me to forgive my dad. That was certainly godly counsel. The problem was, it came across to me as overly simplistic and sounded like a spiritual pat answer. While I am sure this was not my friends' intent, it felt to me as though they were saying that hatred, anger, and bitterness were little "switches" in my heart and that I should just go down there (wherever "there" is) and turn them off. I should simply choose not to be angry, bitter, and resentful. If I would just "give it to Jesus," then everything would be fine.

If anger and bitterness were just switches we could "turn off" with the force of our will, that would be an easy choice to make. But we all know reality is more complicated. I was a twisted mess of emotional and spiritual confusion. I didn't feel ready to forgive my father. He had not asked for forgiveness. I did not have warm feelings for him. He had not done anything to warrant my ever trusting him again.

God used my youth pastor, Ken Geis, to shepherd me through this dark time. Over the course of a few months, he shared with me, from the pages of Scripture, the path of true forgiveness. No pat answers. No quick fixes. No rose-colored glasses. Forgiveness is an intentional process that takes place through God's power and grace, and in it God sets us free from bitterness, anger, and hatred, preparing us for the possibility of reconciliation.

Forgiveness and reconciliation is a three-phase process, and I will summarize it here. I don't want you to be overwhelmed.

What can be written in just a few pages may take years for the Lord to accomplish in us. In the chapters ahead, we will consider the small steps God would have us take toward this vision of family healing.

Three Phases of Forgiveness

Phase 1—Forgiveness with the will

If we are commanded to forgive, then forgiveness must involve a choice. It begins with an act of the will, with obedience to Christ. Forgive as the Lord has forgiven you. At this point, we are confronted with numerous obstacles. *I don't "feel ready" to forgive my brother. My sister has not taken responsibility for her bad behavior. My mother-in-law has not apologized and asked for our forgiveness. Even if I choose to forgive my dad, he is just going to continue with his toxic behavior.* While all those factors are important, and painful, they are not relevant to this first phase of forgiveness. In this phase, feelings are not your friends and can actually keep you from taking a real step toward healing and freedom. If you wait until you "feel ready" to forgive, you may end up waiting your entire life.

How do we take this first step toward forgiving a member of our family? I encourage you to get alone with the Lord for thirty minutes. Take out a sheet of paper and at the top write, "It hurt me when . . ." What you write on this paper will only be for you and the Lord. In fact, when you are done you will throw the paper away.

Ask the Lord to bring to your mind specific things your family member has done or said over the years that have hurt you. As those things come to mind, write them down. It doesn't matter if your list is long or short. Just write down events and moments that hurt you. When your list is complete, choose through prayer to forgive him or her for each individual item.

My prayer regarding my father sounded something like this: "Lord, I know you want me to forgive my father. Honestly, I don't feel ready to do it. He has not asked for forgiveness or acknowledged how much he hurt me and our family. But I know you want me to forgive him so that my heart will be free of hatred and bitterness. So . . . I choose to forgive him for cheating on Mom. I choose to forgive him for putting random women ahead of our family. I choose to forgive . . ."

When you are done, throw the paper away (or burn it if that makes you feel better!).

Here is what happens when we take this first step of forgiveness. Imagine an old wooden bucket. Over the years, your family drops in glops of thick mud. These are the hurts and wounds you have experienced. Now, because your bucket is filled to the rim, any time someone in your house drops in another glop—*boom!* You are so filled with hurt and resentment from the past that any new offense causes everything to overflow. When we make the choice to forgive, it is like taking a hammer and smashing a hole in the bottom of the bucket. When we tear the hammer out, a nice big glop of mud comes out with it. Now, instead of 100 percent full of past hurt and resentment, we are only 95 percent full. As I have counseled hundreds of people through this process, many experience an immediate lightening of their spirit. While it may be only 5 percent, they sense a bit of emotional breathing room, something they haven't felt for a long time.

But we still have a problem. We still have 95 percent of our old bitterness and anger in the bucket. That leads us into phase two.

Phase 2—Forgiveness with the heart

In Matthew 18:35, Jesus calls us to forgive our brother "from the heart." The heart is God's territory. He is the one who has the power to change our hearts. So if we want our hearts changed, we have to ask God to do it. If we want that old bucket drained of all that bitterness, anger, and resentment, we must open our hearts to Him.

The second phase of forgiveness is a daily prayer. Your prayer may sound something like this: "Lord, I have chosen to forgive my dad. It was not easy to do, and I still don't have anything close to warm feelings toward him. I am afraid to do this because I don't want to get hurt again. But I chose to forgive him out of obedience. Now I ask you to heal my heart. I don't want to hate him. I don't want to be filled with anger and resentment. I don't want his bad behavior to poison my life. I ask that you cleanse my heart of all those things so that I can be free . . . free to love you, and even free to love my dad."

I was in phase two for *six years*. It was six years of praying daily, "God, heal my heart. Take away my anger and bitterness." Slowly and mercifully, God drained and cleaned out my old bucket. Later in our journey together I will share how God ultimately replaced my anger and bitterness toward my father with compassion.

Phase 3—Reconciliation

The final phase of forgiveness is when a relationship is healed and reconciled. But here is a hard truth—it is possible for God to bring us to a place of complete forgiveness without the relationship being fully healed. It may be that the family member who has hurt you never repents, never takes responsibility or changes his or her behavior. Reconciliation is not sweeping things under the rug and pretending they never happened. Reconciliation is not enabling or tolerating ongoing abuse. In the upcoming chapters, we will explore what true reconciliation looks like and how the Lord can accomplish it. Our responsibility before the Lord, and to our family, is to do everything in our power, as far as it depends on us, to forgive and to *seek* reconciliation. In Romans 12:18 God says, "*If possible, so far as it depends on you, live peaceably with all.*" We can't control the attitudes and actions of our family members. They may have no interest in forgiveness or reconciliation. But, as far as it depends on us, we can still seek healing.

How Many Times Do I Need to Forgive?

When a family member does something that hurts our feelings a couple of times, it may not feel like a big deal to forgive them. But what if they do it ten times? Fifty times? Now it is a different story. You may remember that Jesus' disciples asked Him about this. "*Then Peter came to him and asked, 'Lord, how often should I forgive someone who sins against me? Seven times?' 'No, not seven times,' Jesus replied, 'but seventy times seven!'*" (Matthew 18:21–22 NLT). Peter probably thought that forgiving his brother seven times for something was quite generous. Jesus blasted that out of the water when He called Peter to forgive seventy times seven. This, of course, was not meant to be a literal number. *Four hundred eighty-eight . . . four hundred eighty-nine . . . almost there!* It was a call to a lifetime and lifestyle of forgiveness.

I once heard a powerful seminar by Jerry Root, a professor at Wheaton College. He emphasized how the call to forgive is first and foremost a choice we make for our own freedom and wholeness. He shared this illustration: If you have rats in your house, you don't get rid of them by eating a box of rat poison. That course of action won't do anything to the rats and might just kill you. Holding on to bitterness and anger hurts us far more than the person with whom we are in conflict. Jerry asked, "How many times should we say no to eating rat poison?"[3] Every time. All the time. "Seventy times seven times." Choosing forgiveness is choosing freedom.

Are You Ready to Take a Step?

The first step toward freedom is making the choice to forgive. Flip back a few pages and reread the section called "Phase 1— Forgiveness with the will." It may take about thirty minutes with the Lord for you to take this first step of obedience. However, for those of us who have experienced significant family trauma, it can take years before the Lord brings us to a place where we are ready or feel able to do this. If that is where you are right now, be honest with yourself and honest with God. But don't stop reading. God loves you, and He will not abandon you. He will make the next step clear, then give you the strength to follow through. I believe the Lord led you to read this book because He wants to begin and accelerate healing in your life.

Perhaps you are ready to take this first action step of forgiveness. Find a quiet time to meet with God and boldly choose to obey His call to forgive. Write your list. Pray through it, then tear it up and throw it away. You have then taken a step on the path toward healing.

Questions for Reflection and Discussion

1. When you were growing up, how did your family handle conflict and family problems?
2. Forgiveness is not easy. What might be holding you back from choosing to take the first step of forgiveness?
3. Which relationship in your family is the most challenging for you right now? Take time and pray specifically for God to bring healing and hope to that relationship.

Chapter 2

Healing through Prayer

But I say to you, Love your enemies and pray for those who persecute you.

Matthew 5:44

Reconciliation. Forgiveness. Healing. Restoration. These are, ultimately, matters of the heart. They are God's territory. These are miracles that He accomplishes. We need God to powerfully move in our hearts, and in the hearts of our family members, if we are to experience true healing. Therefore, we need to pray. My struggle, and maybe you can relate, is that I talk a lot about my need to pray, but I end up praying very little. My good intentions to pray don't always translate into action. The prayer strategies in this chapter will be totally useless unless we put them into practice. Let's learn how to pray, then quickly move into *praying*.

We are going to walk through a prayer plan with six essential biblical components. You can pray through all six of these areas in just a few minutes, or you can focus on one area at a time. Remember, the key is not mastering a prayer formula, but praying. If one of the prayer approaches here is helpful to you, take a break from your reading and put it into practice.

Pray for Your Own Heart

When I am in the middle of a blowout conflict with one of my sons, I am squarely focused on *his* disobedience, *his* bad attitude, *his* irresponsibility. Obviously, the entire reason we are in this situation is that *he* dropped the ball or was disrespectful. Rarely is a family conflict 100 percent the fault of one person and 0 percent the fault of the other. Normally, when two sinful people are in conflict, both have contributed some sin along the way. I have lost track of the number of times I have needed to circle around with one of my children after an argument and ask for their forgiveness for my harshness, impatience, or failure to listen. The conflict may have started with his disobedience, but it was made worse by my anger.

Sometimes my harsh spirit toward my kids is not even the result of something specific they have done wrong but simply

> We need God to powerfully move in our hearts, and in the hearts of our family members, if we are to experience true healing.

behaviors and patterns that annoy me. My seventeen-year-old son, JD, is a man of few words. I, as you might expect, am a man of many words. JD would err on the side of talking too little, and I too much. This personality difference can cause friction in our relationship. This is not an issue of right and wrong. It is easy for me to slip into a mode where the solution to the problem is to get JD to use more words. The more urgent need is for me to pray and ask God to change my heart and give me a spirit of acceptance for JD's more laid-back personality. We too quickly equate personality patterns with character problems.

Some of our conflicts at home stem from simple personality differences, while many are caused by sinful attitudes and actions. We are quick to judge our family members, as we easily see their character problems and bad behavior, yet we are slow to judge ourselves and are often blind to our own toxic attitudes and harmful actions. Jesus challenges each one of us on this common pattern.

> "Why do you see the speck that is in your brother's eye, but do not notice the log that is in your own eye? Or how can you say to your brother, 'Let me take the speck out of your eye,' when there is the log in your own eye? You hypocrite, first take the log out of your own eye, and then you will see clearly to take the speck out of your brother's eye."
>
> Matthew 7:3–5

Jesus doesn't hold back. He goes so far as to say the reality of the situation may be that your brother's sin is far *smaller* than yours. Ouch! But the point here is not trying to figure out who is to blame, or who is more at fault. Jesus wants us to deal with our issues first. The problem is, we all have these things called blind spots, so we need to pray and ask God to open our eyes to see how we have contributed, and are contributing, to the broken relationship. Your prayer may sound something like this:

Lord, I know that my conflict with _____ [the name of your family member] is not all his/her fault. I know I have made things worse with my actions and attitudes. I also admit that I struggle with focusing all my thoughts and feelings on what he/she has done to hurt me. I don't

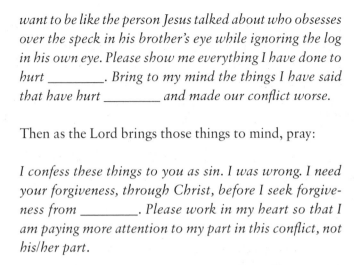

want to be like the person Jesus talked about who obsesses over the speck in his brother's eye while ignoring the log in his own eye. Please show me everything I have done to hurt _____. Bring to my mind the things I have said that have hurt _____ and made our conflict worse.

Then as the Lord brings those things to mind, pray:

I confess these things to you as sin. I was wrong. I need your forgiveness, through Christ, before I seek forgiveness from _____. Please work in my heart so that I am paying more attention to my part in this conflict, not his/her part.

Pray for God to Bless Your Family Member

This prayer strategy is *not easy*, but it is extraordinarily powerful. When we are in conflict with someone, the last thing in the world we want to do is pray for God to bless them. If we are going to pray for them, we are more inclined to echo some of David's prayers in the Psalms when he called on God to smite his enemies! Jesus gave us this challenge in Luke 6:28 (NIV), "*Bless those who curse you, pray for those who mistreat you.*" Then again in Matthew 5:44, "*But I say to you, Love your enemies and pray for those who persecute you.*"

The language here may sound a little harsh. My brother is not my *enemy*. My wife is not *persecuting* me. For others, this language sounds exactly right. It feels like your family member is an enemy right now or has truly abused you. (We will address some of these more extreme situations in chapter 7.) What does Jesus tell us to do? Pray for them. Pray for God to bless them.

I am asking God to help me with this when Amy and I are in conflict. When we are trapped in an argument, I don't naturally pray for God to bless her, I pray for God to fix her. *God, help Amy to understand my perspective on this. Help her with her anger and frustration. Help her communicate in a more positive way with me.* There is nothing wrong with a prayer like this, but it is not the place to start. I need to start by following Jesus' instruction to pray for God to bless her. *Lord, you know that Amy and I are struggling right now. I ask that you would bless her. Give her your peace. Give her your encouragement. Reward her for being such a faithful wife and mother.*

Are you ready to try a blessing prayer for one of your family members? Consider using this pattern as a guide:

Lord, I confess that it is not easy to pray for _____. *But I want to be obedient to Jesus and pray even for those who are mistreating me. So I pray for* _____ *and ask that you would bless him/her. Bless him/her with your presence, your power, and your grace. Bless every area of his/her life. When he/she comes to mind, especially if I am struggling with negative feelings, help me to pray for your blessing in his/her life.*

There are two powerful results from this prayer approach. First, if I pray a blessing prayer for Amy when we are in conflict, it softens my heart toward her. It's hard to pray for God to bless her *and* be angry and bitter at the same time. Second, as God answers my prayer and brings His blessing and presence into Amy's life, that answered prayer can have only a positive effect on our relationship.

Pray for Reconciliation

This one seems obvious, yet we often miss it. We need to pray specifically and directly for God to bring healing to the broken relationship. Perhaps you frequently have thoughts such as, *I wish things were better with me and my father*, or, *I miss the good relationship I used to have with my sister*. I find myself discussing my difficult family relationships with my trusted friends. I share with them my struggles and burden for the relationship, and I ask for their advice and prayers. The sad reality is that I often spend more time talking to friends about the broken relationship than I spend talking to God about it. I spend more time asking my friends to pray for me than actually praying. Jesus invites us to pray plainly and directly when we talk with God:

> "And I tell you, ask, and it will be given to you; seek, and you will find; knock, and it will be opened to you. For everyone who asks receives, and the one who seeks finds, and to the one who knocks it will be opened. What father among you, if his son asks for a fish, will instead of a fish give him a serpent; or if he asks for an egg, will give him a scorpion? If you then, who are evil, know how to give good gifts to your children, how much more will the heavenly Father give the Holy Spirit to those who ask him!"
>
> Luke 11:9–13

The message of Jesus here is not that God is like a genie in a bottle who gives us whatever we want, but rather that God invites our honest, needy prayers. We can be direct with Him. He cares about our greatest and smallest concerns. We can tell Him the desires of our hearts. Is the desire of your heart to see healing in this relationship with your family member? Your ongoing prayer might sound something like this:

Lord, thank you that I can be direct and honest with you. Thank you that you are a good father who cares about the desires of my heart. Right now, my desire is that you would heal my relationship with _____. If I could fix it, I would. But if this relationship is going to be restored, you will have to act. Please bring healing to this relationship. Show me anything I need to do to help this happen and give me the courage to do it.

While we are praying for reconciliation, let's be sure we are not speaking against our own prayers. Consider the wife who

> **God cares about our greatest and smallest concerns.**

has been praying for years for God to soften the heart of her husband, but when she is with her friends she regularly says, "Oh, you know Jim. He will never change." A father is praying regularly for reconciliation with his adult son while at the same time telling his wife, "That kid will never grow up." Instead, ask God to fill your prayers with hope and faith.

Pray with Endurance

This is one of the most difficult and most important aspects of prayer, especially as it relates to broken family relationships. Why doesn't God just fix this (or fix him!)? For some of us, we have been praying for years for healing and reconciliation. Maybe we are just talking to the wall, or God is not listening, or worse, maybe He doesn't even care?

I prayed for my father's salvation and for healing in our relationship for more than thirty years. Over those decades, which began in childhood, there were seasons of intense prayer, seasons of hopelessness, and everything in between. I am convinced God heard all those prayers and saw all those tears.

Let's look more carefully at Luke 11:9: "*And I tell you, ask, and it will be given to you; seek, and you will find; knock, and it will be opened to you.*" Jesus gives us three commands here. *Ask. Seek. Knock.* These are all present-tense commands, which means Jesus wants us to ask, and keep on asking. Seek, and keep on seeking. Knock, and keep on knocking. When it comes to healing broken family relationships, endurance in prayer is essential.

It is amazing that God tells us to pray like this. As a parent, it drives me nuts when my kids ask for things over and over again.

"Dad, can I have another donut?"

"No. One is enough."

Five minutes later. "Dad, I'm still hungry. Can I have another donut?"

"No! I already said no."

Two minutes later. "Hey—how about just half of that chocolate-frosted one?"

"Whatever. Eat the whole thing. Just stop bugging me."

Admittedly, this is not a testimony of great parenting. But repeated asking often *gets results*. It might sound a little sacrilegious to say it this way, but God allows us to nag Him. He *invites* us to nag Him. Jesus told a parable in Luke 18 to encourage us to pray with persistence and endurance. The story was about a widow who continued to plead her case to an uncaring and prideful judge. He continually refused her pleas for justice, yet she kept coming to him with her request. Finally, the judge granted her the ruling she was seeking because he was fed up with her incessant pestering.

Jesus then said, "*Will not God give justice to his elect, who cry to him day and night? Will he delay long over them? I tell you, he will give justice to them speedily*" (Luke 18:7–8).

35

The point here is not that God is an arrogant judge who only answers the prayers of those who pester Him, but rather that if a corrupt judge responds to persistent requests, how much more will our good and loving Father in heaven respond? This is clear in the introduction to the story: *"And he told them a parable to the effect that they ought always to pray and not lose heart"* (Luke 18:1).

You are not bothering God with your continual prayers. You are not annoying Him. He loves you. He invites your "broken record" pleas. He welcomes the needy, repetitive, constant prayers of His children. Let us pray and not lose heart.

Pray Together

The first four prayer strategies have been personal in that they haven't directly involved the family member with whom we are in conflict. We can do each of these within our personal relationship with God. If it is possible to pray together with your family member, I strongly encourage you to try it. I understand this may not be possible. Your relationship may be so broken that all communication has been cut off. It may be that your family member is not walking in a relationship with God or that they simply have no interest in or desire to pray with you. However, if you believe there is a chance that your sibling, spouse, parent, or child would be willing to pray with you, either in person or over the phone, go for it!

Amy and I recently celebrated twenty-five years of marriage together, and like most couples, we have our fair share of conflict. But one area where God has helped us to improve as a couple is that we are more quickly turning to prayer when arguments heat up. We are having a conflict about who knows what, emotions are starting to flare, and one of us (through gritted teeth) says, "Hey—before this gets worse, I think we should pray." Grrrr. In those moments, praying is the last thing I want to do! Prayer requires that I humble myself. Prayer requires that I lower the walls of my heart, both to the Lord and to Amy. So we push the pause button on our argument and hold hands. In that moment, it is like holding a cold, dead fish. I often begin with something like, "Lord, help us . . ." Just three needy words. I have lost track of the number of times Amy and I have gone to God in the midst of conflict—asking for His help—and seen the Holy Spirit rush in and soften my heart toward her and her heart toward me. And then He provides us with a path out of our anger and struggle.

What do you think will happen if you and your family member go before God together and ask for His help and healing in your relationship? He will surely help you. Consider saying something like this to your family member, either in person or over the phone:

> "I know it has been rough in our relationship for a while. I wish things were better between us, and you probably do too. This may sound weird or uncomfortable, but would it be okay if we took a minute and prayed together? If things are going to get any better, we need God's power and help. Would it be all right if I prayed for us?"

Asking to pray together requires tremendous courage. Know that the demons are going to battle you on this one. Therefore, be strong and stand firm! If your family member is willing to pray with you, perhaps your prayer could sound something like this:

> *Lord, you know all about the struggles in our relationship. We have really messed things up, and sometimes it seems like the more we try to fix it, the worse it gets. We need your power to change our hearts and heal our relationship*

*and our family. You know what we need more than we do.
You know what needs to change in our hearts. Help us. We
ask for your power to strengthen and heal our relationship.*

Warning! If God gives you the opportunity to pray *with* your
family member, stay far away from any kind of prayer for God
to fix him or her. "Lord, I ask that you work in my sister's heart
so that she becomes a more loving person." This kind of prayer
will do more harm than good.

Pray for God to Make Himself Look Good

This sixth prayer component is one that God particularly loves.
Let's pray that God would make himself look good through the
struggle and healing of our family relationships. The biblical
concept here is that we want God to *glorify* himself. We want
Him to reveal himself, to show off His power, to act in such a
way that people see it and praise Him for His goodness.

This is the power of *testimonies*. When we hear someone's
conversion story, about how God brought them from darkness into light, from death to life, we don't come away saying,
"Wow—what an amazing person. He pulled himself up by his
bootstraps and really made something of his life." No, we say,
"God is good! His love and His power are amazing. No one
is beyond His ability to save and redeem." A *story of healing*
makes God look good.

Earlier I shared about my relationship with JD. During his
middle teen years, there was tension in our relationship. Many
factors contributed to this. I was exasperating him by treating
him like a child rather than a teen moving toward adulthood. He
struggled to communicate with me and at times was disrespectful. We were also dealing with the normal roller coaster of teen
life and emotions. JD and I talked often about our relationship

because we both wanted it to be better. For almost two years, as I met with my prayer partners from church, my relationship with JD was always high on my list of prayer requests. I asked these men, dozens of times, "Keep praying for JD and me. Pray for God to soften our hearts toward each other. Pray for God to give me wisdom as a dad and not exasperate him. We are working on our relationship, but we need a breakthrough from the Lord." Amy prayed for us more than anyone.

It was around Christmastime of JD's junior year of high school when the hundreds of prayers began to bear fruit. Our relationship felt easier. Our communication calmed and increased. We spent more time together having fun as well as working. Just last week JD said to me, "Dad, I think our relationship is ten times better than before." Amen! How did this happen? First and foremost, prayer. God did it. Did JD work hard on his side of the relationship? Yes. Did I do the same? Yes. But the breakthrough we have experienced was God's doing. For many weeks now, I have been able to tell my prayer partners, "Things are going much better in my relationship with JD. God is answering your prayers. Please keep praying for us." God's work in JD's and my relationship makes *Him* look good.

When you pray for the broken relationship in your family, remember that there is more at stake than "patching things up" in that specific conflict. This is a situation through which God can show off His love and power. Consider praying along these lines:

Lord, I know you love to take broken things and make them whole. I know you love to take dead things and make them live. I am asking you to heal this broken relationship I have with _____. Not only do I want you to heal this relationship for our sakes, but I also know that if you do this, you will look good! I will give you all the credit for this miracle. This will be a "God story" we will tell for generations to come!

Stop Talking and Start Praying

Here are the six prayer strategies we explored in this chapter:

- Pray for your own heart
- Pray for God to bless your family member
- Pray for reconciliation
- Pray with endurance
- Pray together
- Pray for God to make himself look good

You now have a game plan for your prayer strategy. It is time to execute. Which one of these six approaches will you start with? Here are some action strategies to help you:

- Write down reminders to pray. For many of us "out of sight, out of mind" is how we tend to function, so put a Post-it note on your mirror or next to the coffeemaker that reads, "Pray for family healing." When you see the note, take a few seconds and pray.
- Ask for accountability. Tell a friend that you want to be praying more faithfully for a difficult family relationship, but that you need help and encouragement. Invite them to call, text, or email you weekly to encourage you to pray and not lose heart.
- Use your tech. Create a recurring daily appointment or notification reminder on your smartphone or computer, "Pray for family healing." When this pops up, stop what you're doing and pray.

- Just start again. If you are like me, you will pray faithfully for a few days, but then fall off the plan. Start again. Praying inconsistently is infinitely more powerful than not praying at all.

- Start now. My hope is that you have already periodically stopped reading as you have gone through this chapter to talk with God. If not, don't go on to the next chapter. Instead, flip back a few pages and use the sample prayers to guide your conversation with the Lord. He is listening. You have His full-and-undivided attention.

Questions for Reflection and Discussion

1. Pick one of the prayer strategies as a starting point. Which did you choose and why?
2. What are some of the barriers keeping you from praying faithfully for this broken family relationship?
3. In what ways could God make himself look good through your difficult situation? How could your family story be used to point others to Him?
4. Do you think your family member would be willing to pray *with* you, asking together for God's help and healing? If yes, when would be a good time to ask him/her to pray with you?

Chapter 3

Healing through Repentance

> Or do you presume on the riches of his kindness and forbearance and patience, not knowing that God's kindness is meant to lead you to repentance?
>
> Romans 2:4

Family conflicts start very early in life. Ray (age nine) and Milly (age eleven) were working on cleaning the kitchen together. They began to argue over who would do what job. Ray wanted to wipe the counter. Milly wanted him to clear the table. Milly, as the older sister, shifted into "boss mode" and harshly issued her orders. Rush (age five) was playing with his toys in the next room and could hear what was going on between his siblings in the kitchen. Rush shouted, "Milly, say, 'I'm sorry'! Milly, you need to say, 'I'm sorry'!" He said it four times. Milly finally received his advice and said, "Ray, I'm sorry." Then Rush shouted, "Now, Ray, you say, 'I forgive you'!" Ray followed instructions. Opportunities for repentance and forgiveness come early and often.

As we learned in the previous chapter, family conflicts are rarely one-sided, with all of the fault resting on just one person. Even if the problem we're having with a family member is *mostly* their fault, we have likely contributed to the situation with our words, actions, and attitudes. To whatever degree we have sinned, hurt someone, or caused a conflict to worsen, we can pursue healing of that relationship through *repentance*.

It is not easy to focus on our part in a family conflict. We quickly and clearly see all the things our brother has done over the years, and continues to do, to hurt us. Our vision is far less clear to identify—and our spirit far less eager to take responsibility for—our own sins.

Maybe you have thought something like, *He should apologize first! As soon as he apologizes, then I will apologize.* Many family conflicts hit a roadblock at this point. Who should be the first to apologize? At a seminar, I heard Dr. Emerson Eggerichs answer the question this way: "The more mature person should apologize first."[1] That was a winsome and convicting way to encourage each of us to take the lead in confessing and seeking forgiveness. The Lord gives us a gentle challenge on this point in Romans 12:18: "*If possible, so far as it depends on you, live peaceably with all.*" You can't control whether your mother will seek peace in her relationship with you, but you can still seek peace in your relationship with her.

Repentance Begins with a Change of Mind

Repentance is a churchy word. Sometimes we use religious words without understanding their actual meaning. In the Bible, particularly the New Testament, the word *repentance* literally means "a change of mind." It means that we radically shift our thinking, attitude, and mind-set about our sin. We take responsibility and drop the excuses. We stop sugarcoating, minimizing, and blaming.

I can think of situations when I have lost my temper with Amy. I went to her and said, "I am sorry I yelled at you, but I would not have gotten angry if you had not spoken disrespectfully to me." Rather than take full responsibility for my anger and harshness, I blamed my wife. Repentance is a complete *changing* of the mind. Instead of passing the buck, I fully accept that the buck stops with me.

Repentance Continues with a Change in Behavior

True repentance does not stop with a change in our thinking, but continues with a change in our behavior. We have all known people who apologize to us over and over for the same offense, and yet their behavior never changes. After a while, the apologies begin to ring hollow.

Imagine that you are out for a long hike in the woods. After walking for a while, you recognize that you have taken a wrong turn. You stop hiking in the wrong direction, turn around, and hike back toward the point where you took the wrong turn. That is repentance. First, you recognize that you have gone down the wrong path (your mind changes). Second, you turn around and take intentional steps in the right direction (your behavior changes).

The Example of Joseph's Brothers

A powerful picture of family healing is found in the account of Joseph and his brothers. Joseph was the eleventh brother out of twelve. He was favored by Jacob, his father, and his older brothers were jealous of him—so much so that they sold him into slavery and told their father he had been devoured by wild animals. In Egypt, after many years, God delivered Joseph from slavery and elevated him to serve as Pharaoh's second-in-command. God enabled Joseph to save the Egyptian people from an extended period of famine. However, the famine spread to Israel, and Joseph's family was starving. Joseph's father sent his ten older brothers to Egypt to buy food. They appeared before Joseph but did not recognize him. Was there any hope for healing, forgiveness, and reconciliation? Joseph needed to know if his brothers had changed or if they were the same selfish, angry, jealous men who had sold him into slavery.

Joseph devised a way to test them. He accused them of being spies and had them detained. He told them he would believe their story if they would return home and bring Benjamin, the youngest brother, back to Egypt. This was a moment of crisis and panic for the ten brothers as they recalled their sin against Joseph.

> Then they said to one another, "In truth we are guilty concerning our brother, in that we saw the distress of his soul, when he begged us and we did not listen. That is why this distress has come upon us." And Reuben answered them, "Did I not tell you not to sin against the boy? But you did not listen. So now there comes a reckoning for his blood." They did not know that Joseph understood them, for there was an interpreter between them.
>
> Genesis 42:21–23

What a powerful moment. The brothers, thinking they were having a private conversation, said to one another, "*In truth we are guilty concerning our brother.*" Joseph saw a sign of repentance! Their minds had changed. They made no excuses for what they had done. Reuben was blunt enough to simply call it sin. Joseph, seeing his brothers' repentant hearts, left the room and wept. Nine of the brothers returned home to get Benjamin while

45

Simeon remained in custody in Egypt. The brothers returned to Egypt with Benjamin, but Joseph had one more test for them.

> [Joseph] commanded the steward of his house, "Fill the men's sacks with food, as much as they can carry, and put each man's money in the mouth of his sack, and put my cup, the silver cup, in the mouth of the sack of [Benjamin], with his money for the grain." And he did as Joseph told him.
>
> Genesis 44:1–2

When the "stolen" items were discovered, the brothers were brought back to Joseph. They were terrified, and rightly so, that Benjamin would be imprisoned or executed. Years ago, these ten men callously discarded the life of their younger brother Joseph. What would they do now with their youngest brother, Benjamin?

Repentance is a change in thinking that leads to a change in behavior. The brothers had changed their thinking about what they had done to Joseph. They had taken responsibility. They had called it sin. But would they *act differently* in regard to Benjamin? Yes! Judah took the lead in pleading with Joseph for Benjamin's life, explaining what would happen if they returned home to Jacob without Benjamin.

> "As soon as he sees that the boy is not with us, he will die, and your servants will bring down the gray hairs of your servant our father with sorrow to Sheol. For your servant became a pledge of safety for the boy to my father, saying, 'If I do not bring him back to you, then I shall bear the blame before my father all my life.' Now therefore, please let your servant remain instead of the boy as a servant to my lord, and let the boy go back with his brothers. For how can I go back to my father if the boy is not with me? I fear to see the evil that would find my father."
>
> Genesis 44:31–34

Judah offered his own life to save Benjamin! This was true repentance. It was at this moment that the floodgates of healing and reconciliation opened. Joseph could no longer control

> ## Repentance is a change in thinking that leads to a change in behavior.

himself, cleared the room, and through many tears announced his true identity to his brothers. God then brought about a miraculous healing, reconciliation, and a family reunion.

Repentance in Action

Remember, this is an *action* book more than a *learning* book. To act on this call to repentance, we need to engage vertically and horizontally. A portion of our repentance work needs to be done with God, and a portion of it needs to be done with our family member. Confession is an essential and early action step in repentance. To *confess* means "to say with" or "to agree with." When we confess a sin to God, we are telling God that He is right and we are wrong. We are *agreeing* with Him and His Word that something we have done or said is sin. Why should we even bother to confess our sins to God? Consider this extraordinary promise from the Lord.

> If we say we have no sin, we deceive ourselves, and the truth is not in us. If we confess our sins, he is faithful and just to forgive us our sins and to cleanse us from all unrighteousness.
>
> 1 John 1:8–9

Christ has paid the full price for all our sins, and therefore forgiveness is freely offered to us. Amen! But confession requires specificity. We do not pray, "Lord, I want to confess the sins I have committed today. I can't remember any of them in particular, but I am sure you do, so I want to ask for a general forgiveness of those miscellaneous sins." No! When we confess our sins, we name them. "Lord, I confess my sin of gossip today. I was wrong to share private information about my friend with those people. I am sorry. Thank you for forgiving me through Jesus. I don't want to keep doing this. Change my heart. Help me not to betray my friend's trust again."

Repentance with the Lord

Let's get to work. Consider your strained relationship with your family member. In the previous chapter, you prayed and asked the Lord to bring to mind the things you have done to damage the relationship. Take a moment now and write those things down. Once you have your list, bring each item to God in a spirit of repentance. Your prayer might sound something like this:

Lord, I admit that my broken relationship with _____ is not all his/her fault. I have sinned against him/her. I want to repent of all those sins right now.

I confess my sin of _____.

I fully admit I was wrong when I _____.

I take responsibility for _____.

Thank you that I can confess all these things to you because of Jesus' death and resurrection. Thank you for your forgiveness through Christ. Not only do I confess these things to you, but I want you to change my heart and my behavior. I don't want to do more damage to this relationship. Yet my behavior will not change unless you change my heart and empower me to live differently.

Repentance with Our Family Member

After we have done the vertical work of repentance, it is time to do the horizontal work of repentance and confession with our family member. You may be in a situation in which you have no personal contact with your brother or your mother. In that case, do the vertical work of repentance and then ask the Lord to prepare your heart for the day in the future when He may make it possible for you to talk about these things personally with your family member.

Repentance is more than an apology. Too often, apologies are superficial exchanges of "the right words." This starts in childhood. I can remember a particular recess time in the third grade. All the boys were out on the playground, and I got into a fracas with one of the boys about whether he was safe or out at second base in our kickball game. We started yelling and pushing, and quickly a teacher came over to break it up. The teacher separated us and said, "You boys need to say you're sorry!" I stared at the boy. He stared back. I mumbled, "Sorrrry." He sarcastically replied, "Sooorrryyy." The teacher then patted us on the heads and replied, "Good boys! Now go back and play." Let's be honest about what happened here. Yes, out of both of our mouths came the word *sorry*, or syllables approximating it. What we truly said was, "I hate your guts. Just wait until the teacher is gone!" But because we both had said the magic word *sorry*, somehow that made everything okay. Apologies can be superficial and fake. Repentance and confession are real.

A Five-Step Conversation

There are five powerful ingredients we can include when we ask for forgiveness from a family member. Before you share these things, it may be helpful to begin your conversation this way: "I want to have an important conversation with you. I know we have been dealing with problems in our relationship, and I want you to know that some of those problems are my fault. I have some things I want to confess to you."

Step 1: Confession

Confession should be short and sweet. We simply state the wrong thing we did.

"I was rude to you."
"I yelled at you."
"I was jealous of you."
"I neglected you."
"I cheated on you."
"I slapped you."
"I have been looking at porn."
"I lied to you about our money situation."

If it is a list of things, go through the list. No sugarcoating. No blaming. No excuses. Just clearly admit what you did. This means battling through any shame we may feel. I remember a time when I spilled a large glass of water all over one of my books. I needed to get the book dried out quickly, so I had the brilliant idea of putting the book in the microwave. I cranked the thing up, and after a minute or so, the book caught on fire. It burned in there for a few seconds, and then after a loud *bang*, the microwave shut down. I quickly opened the microwave, grabbed the book, and threw it in the sink. There was smoke everywhere, and the microwave was shot. Amy was out, and I got everything cleaned up. When she came home, she smelled the smoke and asked what had happened. I lied and said, "I was heating up my dinner in the microwave and accidentally left my fork on the plate. The metal fork started sparking and caused the microwave to blow." I was ashamed of my foolishness, so I tried to cover it up with a lie. Eventually, the truth came out, but I had done additional damage to the situation by failing to quickly confess the truth.

Step 2: Acknowledge you were wrong

This is an extraordinarily powerful sentence when it comes from the heart. After you have confessed your sins, simply say, "I was wrong." Here are three words many people seem incapable of expressing. No one likes to admit to being wrong. Our pride is like a cork in our mouths that prevents these words from escaping. In my experience, I am only able to honestly say this if I have done the needed vertical work of repentance. I need the Lord to soften my heart and break my pride so that I can truly humble myself before my family.

Step 3: Express regret

This is the step where we say, "I am sorry." But there may be value in digging deeper. What are we sorry for? Are we sorry we got caught? Are we sorry for the annoying conflict? For me, when the Lord gives me a truly repentant heart, I am sorry—I feel bad—for how my words and actions hurt my family member. I am not "sorry this happened," but I am "sorry that I hurt you." You might say, "I know that my selfishness hurt you, and I am very sorry for that," or "I feel terrible that my lies have hurt you and caused you not to trust me. I am sorry."

Step 4: Commit to change

Repentance is a change of mind that leads to a change in behavior. While we cannot promise (or deliver) on a perfect future, we can express our desire to change our future behavior. "I want you to know I have confessed these things to God. I have asked the Lord, and will continue to ask Him, to change my heart and help me to act differently." In some situations, it may be necessary to take additional steps to clarify your commitment to pursuing change. "I have made the decision to start counseling with my pastor/Christian counselor," or "I will be talking each week with [person's name], who I have asked to help keep me accountable to making changes in this area of my life."

Step 5: Ask for forgiveness

The prayerful goal of this process is that your family member will make the choice to forgive you for what you have done to contribute to the conflict. If they choose to forgive you, that does not mean all difficult feelings will be instantly erased. However, asking for, giving, and receiving forgiveness are powerful steps on the path toward healing and reconciliation.

After you have walked through the first four steps, consider saying something like, "I want to ask you a question. It is okay if you need time to think about this before you give me an answer. Will you forgive me for what I have done?"

At this point in the conversation, many things can happen. Anger. Tears. Silence. There is nothing you can do to manage the response. You are there to do *your* part. Lord willing, your conversation will be one of many important moments in the healing of the relationship.

How to Make Things Worse

The goal with this courageous action step of repentance is to seek peace by taking a step toward healing the relationship with your family member. But if we are not careful, we can cause additional damage, even with good intentions. Here are some pitfalls to avoid:

I was wrong, but . . .

After we apologize, we often flip things back onto the other person. "I am sorry I lied to you, *but you* have been so angry with me lately and I didn't want to make you more upset." Or, "I was wrong to lose my temper like that, *but you* have a short fuse too!" The first half of each of these sentences is right on the money, but then they take a negative turn with the words *but you*. It may be appropriate to address your family member's behavior, but that is for a different conversation—most likely on a different day.

Aren't you going to apologize?

Sometimes, when my heart is angry and defensive, I apologize for something I did wrong with the secret motive of wanting my family member to apologize *to me*. So I go ahead and apologize and ask for forgiveness (as quickly as possible) and then wait with eager expectation, as if to say, "Well? Don't *you* have something you need to say to me?" If your brother chooses to respond to your repentance with a confession of his own, that is an extra blessing in the conversation. However, it is a much wiser course to simply focus on taking responsibility for your part in the conflict and seeking his forgiveness. Don't press him or demand an apology. Allow the Holy Spirit to bring conviction to him in His time.

Overapologizing

It is possible to take too much responsibility in a strained relationship. We absolutely should take responsibility for the things we have done wrong, yet we can damage the relationship by apologizing beyond that. This can be a pattern in emotionally abusive relationships.

Trevor and Suzanne were experiencing ongoing conflict with their only child, Julia. When Julia was growing up, both her parents were focused on their careers and therefore spent little time with her. The time they did spend with her was focused on her schoolwork and preparation for college. Her grades and test scores were top priority. Trevor and Suzanne "succeeded." Julia ranked high in her class and was accepted into a prestigious university. But by the end of Julia's first year of college, her priorities had shifted from her education to partying. Her alcohol use moved from recreational to addictive. She lost her drive and ability to stay on top of her schoolwork. By the middle of her sophomore year, she had dropped out of school and moved in with her boyfriend.

Whenever Trevor and Suzanne tried to talk with her, she vented her anger over her childhood. She claimed she was neglected, abandoned, and ignored. She accused them of caring only about her grades, not about her as a person. It was many months before her parents were able to see that some of what she was saying was true. They had not built a heart-connected relationship with her. They had put their careers first. God gave them a spirit of repentance. They humbled themselves and confessed these things to the Lord, then to Julia. They did not mince words in their confession to their daughter, which was followed by their asking for her forgiveness. The conversation seemingly had no effect. Julia stormed out. Two weeks later, they wrote her a long letter, reiterating their apology. After getting the letter, Julia texted, "I got the letter. I don't think you are sorry."

Months went by with the family locked in this pattern. The parents kept trying to apologize. Julia continued to reject them. Finally, through help from a counselor, Trevor and Suzanne realized that it was now unhealthy and unproductive for them to continue to apologize. It was right for them to genuinely confess and communicate their sorrow to Julia about their failures as parents, even to do this multiple times. But now Julia was using this pattern to inappropriately punish her parents. She held the power as she waited for her parents to apologize sufficiently. Trevor and Suzanne made the decision to stop apologizing. They assured Julia that they loved her, wanted a good relationship with her, and were looking forward to the day when she could forgive them.

Repentance along the Way

In healthy relationships, conversations like these don't happen once a decade, but more like once a week. Jesus encourages us to address broken relationships without delay.

> "So if you are offering your gift at the altar and there remember that your brother has something against you, leave your gift there before the altar and go. First be reconciled to your brother, and then come and offer your gift."
>
> Matthew 5:23–24

In this passage, Jesus is speaking about a person who wants to worship and follow God. Specifically, this person has come to the temple with an offering and then remembers his conflict with

**Pursuing reconciliation
is an act of worship.**

a brother, that something he did has offended his brother. Jesus calls the man to leave the gift at the altar and first seek peace with his brother. Pursuing reconciliation is an act of worship.

God would have us keep short accounts with one another so that seeds of bitterness do not take root and later grow to cause trouble. The Lord challenges us, "*Be angry and do not sin; do not let the sun go down on your anger, and give no opportunity to the devil"* (Ephesians 4:26–27). God calls us to deal with sin and conflict quickly. Today is the best day to deal with today's problems.

Questions for Reflection and Discussion

1. A spirit of repentance is a gift from God. It does not come naturally. Before considering the remaining questions, ask the Lord for this special gift.
2. Set aside time to consider the specific ways you have contributed to the problems in your relationship with your family member, and to bring those things to the Lord in a spirit of repentance.
3. Think back to your family environment when you were growing up. How was conflict dealt with? What did apologies look like?
4. What fears or anxieties do you have about repenting to your family member and taking responsibility for your part in the conflict?
5. If you are preparing to have a repentance conversation with your family member, is there someone you can ask to provide prayer support for you before and during the conversation?

Chapter 4

Healing through Listening

The ear that listens to life-giving reproof will dwell among the wise.

Proverbs 15:31

Listen to your father who gave you life, and do not despise your mother when she is old.

Proverbs 23:22

I was counseling a twenty-one-year-old man regarding his strained relationship with his father when he said, "Rob, my dad said that he wants to take me out to breakfast tomorrow morning to have a conversation with me. Now, when my dad says he wants to have a conversation, what he means is that he wants to lecture me for an hour about all the things going wrong in my life." He prepared himself to have breakfast with his dad, but he was completely closed-off to anything his dad might say to him. Why? Because he was feeling hurt and disrespected by his father's chronic lack of listening.

"You just don't get it. I don't think you will ever understand me." Have you ever heard words like this from a family member? These words are an indication of a structural flaw in the foundation of the relationship. These words come from a deep place of frustration and are infused with an attitude of hopelessness. When we feel that someone won't even make an effort to listen to and understand our perspective, why should we bother trying to work on the relationship?

Have you ever given your full-and-undivided attention to listening to a small child? Once toddlers get to talking, they can ramble on from one subject to the next. Have you ever locked eyes with that child and fully listened? Did you notice, in that moment, how much the child enjoyed talking with you? The child feels your love, simply through your active and engaged listening.

I remember an incident when my son Rush was two years old. I was holding him while I was walking around the house. In my left hand I had my phone and was scrolling through email, the news, and whatever else. Rush was talking up a storm, as much as a two-year-old can, and I was responding with, "Yeah, uh-huh. Yeah, uh-huh. . . ." Truth be told, I wasn't listening to anything he was saying, because I was lost in my phone. When Rush realized what was going on, he reached up and grabbed my cheeks, pulled my face away from my phone, and firmly said, "Daddy, please look at my eyes when I am talking to you." I wonder where he heard that. I want to be the kind of father who gives his children his full attention and *listens* to them when they are talking.

God Shows Love by Listening

Have you ever considered what an amazing thing it is that God *listens* to you when you talk to Him in prayer? He gives you His full, personal attention. He is able to do the same for billions of people simultaneously. My brain starts to fry if even two people try talking to me at the same time. The Psalmist writes this in Psalm 66:19–20, "*But truly God has listened; he has attended to the voice of my prayer. Blessed be God, because he has not*

> The Creator of the universe
> personally listens to us
> because He loves us.

rejected my prayer or removed his steadfast love from me!" The Creator of the universe personally listens to us because He loves us. Listening is a powerful way of loving.

Being Quick to Listen

Consider this powerful challenge from the Lord: "*Know this, my beloved brothers: let every person be quick to hear, slow to speak, slow to anger; for the anger of man does not produce the righteousness of God*" (James 1:19–20). God's instruction here is completely contrary to my nature. I am quick to speak and slow to listen. I often catch myself, while in a conversation with a friend or family member, while they are speaking, giving half of my attention to what they are saying while the other half of my brain is formulating what I am going to say as soon as they are done.

A few months ago, Amy came to me and said, "Rob, I need to talk to you about something, and I would like to ask you not to interrupt me. Just listen until I am finished, okay?" I was a bit taken aback by her request. "Honey, you don't have to *ask* me not to interrupt you. You can feel free to share whatever you want, and I will just listen." Well, thirty seconds into her speaking, I felt responses, pushback, and correction coming up through my vocal cords. This happened at the one-minute mark as well. Then it dawned on me. Amy had to ask me not to interrupt her because I had a habit of interrupting her. It was a huge blind spot for me. I need to actively ask the Lord to help me reverse my instincts of being quick to speak and slow to listen and apply His command to be quick to listen and slow to speak. Another area where the Lord is growing me is recognizing that just because I'm thinking something doesn't mean I have to say it. I am a verbal processor. That means I work through problems by talking out loud (even to myself, if necessary). In some ways, this is a positive character trait, but it can also work against me and hurt my relationships if I am doing too much talking and not enough listening. Your family members may increasingly push you away if communication feels to them like a one-way street.

Ask for Insight

This is not an easy challenge, but it may bring about significant healing in your family relationships. Ask a few of your family members some of the following questions. You may need to prepare them with a little preamble: "I want to talk with you about something. It's a little awkward and kind of personal, so please bear with me. I am concerned that I might have some blind spots in how I relate to people, so I was hoping that you could honestly answer a couple of questions." After the preamble, here are some questions to consider asking:

- "Would you say that I have a habit of interrupting people when they are talking to me?"
- "When you, or other people in our family, are talking to me, do you feel as though I listen with my full attention?"

- "Do you think I am a person who tries to understand other people's perspectives, or am I too focused on just sharing mine?"

After your family member shares their answers with you, consider just saying, "Thank you for sharing that with me. I'm going to think about what you said." Or, if the situation warrants, you could ask them for more insight. "You said that I don't always do a great job giving people my full attention when they're talking to me. Can you give me an example of that, or maybe a time I did that to you, so I can better understand?" It may be that your family member affirms that you do have an unhealthy pattern of interrupting or not fully listening. If that is the case, it would be an important step of healing to receive and affirm what is being shared with you. "Thank you for being honest with me. I think you're right that I do have a problem with this. I want to grow in this area, and I will be asking God to work in my heart and change my behavior."

Reflective Listening

Sometimes broken and unhealthy communication patterns become locked in, and no matter how many times we try to talk with our family member, it ends badly. For many years, Amy and I had an annual conflict in the weeks leading up to Christmas. It had to do with the volume of gifts and the Christmas budget. My approach was to set a total budget number, and everything related to Christmas needed to stay within the limits of that number. Amy's approach was to set a budget number, but if there were things she would already be buying for the kids, such as new clothes from the clothing budget, then those items could be wrapped up and given on Christmas. I saw this as overspending on Christmas, while she saw it as a way to make

Christmas more special by combining existing budget lines. You may think this is small potatoes, but it tapped into deeper issues for both of us. She grew up with big Christmases. Her love language is gifts. I came into the conversation with anxiety about our overall financial situation. Because we often failed to share our underlying emotions and values, and because we were more focused on getting our own points across (i.e., winning), we experienced years of conflict.

If you find yourself going through the same script in every conversation, you may need to use an intentional tool that can help break you out of the old cycle. This tool is called *reflective listening*. The purpose of this tool is to improve your listening and deepen your understanding. Read through the process below. If you think it would be helpful in your next conversation with your sister, consider showing this page to her. Tell her that you want to do a better job of listening to her and understanding her perspective and that you would like to give this tool a shot.

Step 1: Give your full attention to listening

Your body language can communicate interest or disinterest. Don't slouch or stare off into space. Orient your body and your eyes toward your sister so she knows you are actively listening. Put your phone on silent, or better yet, turn it off. Only check your phone if there is an important reason to do so. In that case, say, "I am sorry. I want to keep listening to you, but I need to check this in case it's urgent."

Step 2: When your family member is done talking, reflect back a summary of what you heard

"If I heard you correctly, you are saying A, B, and C. Is that right?" If your sister feels that you have properly understood what she is saying, move on to step 3. If not, then say, "Okay, please keep talking so that I can understand what you are trying to say." Repeat this process until your sister feels that you understand.

Step 3: Pursue additional understanding

If your sister indicates that you have rightly understood what she is trying to say in her first round of sharing, take the opportunity to dive deeper. You can ask, "Is there more that you want to say about this? I want to make sure you have a chance to share everything that is important to you." If your sister then has more to share, listen carefully and "reflect" her words back to her as explained in step 2.

Step 4: Thank them for sharing and create a plan for the next conversation

When a relationship is broken, healing takes multiple conversations. It may be wise to conclude your conversation by saying, "Thank you for being honest with me. I think I better understand your thoughts and feelings about this. I am going to think carefully about what you said. When do you think would be a good time to continue this conversation?" It is in the next conversation that God may allow you to share things that are on your heart, and give your family member the grace to listen.

Some Do's and Don'ts When Listening[1]

Look for a good time to talk

I am the kind of person who wants things fixed right away. Because of that, I often try to have personal conversations in places or at times that do more harm than good. For example, I will want to work something out with Amy, and because of my impatience I will open a can of relational worms in front of the kids when it would have been far wiser for me to say,

"Amy, there's something I'd like to talk with you about, but in private. Is there a time in the next few hours when we could come together to do that?"

Don't ask combative questions or make blaming statements

The goal of this whole process is to create more warmth, closeness, and understanding in the relationship. If Amy chooses to open up and talk to me, the last thing I want to do is make her regret doing so. Responses like these will probably do more harm than good:

- "Why did you do that?"
- "I just can't understand where you are coming from."
- "I am trying to listen, but you are not being clear."
- "It is so frustrating trying to have a conversation with you."

Don't focus on disagreement

Your wife might say a lot of things you don't agree with. Her facts might be wrong. Her feelings might be misplaced. Her accusations of you might be unfair. God may provide a time to deal with all of that—but not now. In this first conversation, you are pursuing a small step toward healing the relationship with her through listening.

Stay focused on the goal

You have one goal here. You want to understand your family member's perspective, and you will know that you have achieved your goal when *she* expresses to you that *she* thinks you understand. The golden words you are looking to hear from her at the end of this conversation (or series of conversations) are "I feel like you understand me. You get where I am coming from. Thanks for taking the time to listen."

Express gratitude

In the same way that it was probably not easy for you to get this conversation started, it was likely not easy for your family member to share with you. She took a risk in being honest with you. This is a key moment to affirm that. "I know it is not easy for us to talk, so it means a lot to me that you were willing to have this conversation and be honest with me. I want to have a better relationship with you."

A Final Challenge

Listening is a big deal because it is one of the essential ways we show love to our family members. A failure to listen is a failure to love. Not only can a failure to listen hinder our relationships with our family, but it can also affect our relationship with God. Consider God's call to husbands: "*Likewise, husbands, live with your wives in an understanding way, showing honor to the woman as the weaker vessel, since they are heirs with you of the grace of life, so that your prayers may not be hin-*

A failure to listen is a failure to love.

dered" (1 Peter 3:7). First, God commands a husband to live in an "understanding way" with his wife. As we have already discussed, understanding requires listening. Second, notice the warning at the end of the verse. What is the consequence for a husband who fails to seek understanding of his wife and who fails to show her honor? His prayers will be hindered. I don't fully comprehend how this spiritual principle works, yet it appears that if a husband is not inclined to listen to his wife, then God is not inclined to listen to him. We should all take heed of this warning! Learning to listen is not only needed as we seek healing in our family relationships, but also as we seek to walk in a daily relationship with God.

Questions for Reflection and Discussion

1. Consider your home when you were growing up. Who was a good listener? How did that person's commitment to listening affect their relationships with other family members?

2. Take some time to think about the reality that God, the Creator of the universe, chooses to listen to you when you talk with Him in prayer. What does that tell you about God? What does that tell you about His love for you?

3. Do you have a habit of interrupting or not actively listening when your family members are speaking? Confess that to the Lord. Look for an opportunity to confess it to your family members as well.

4. When we have a strained relationship with a family member, we feel awkward and insecure trying to initiate any kind of personal conversation with them. As you think about any difficult relationships you have in your family right now, ask God to give you the courage to open up a conversation with the singular goal of *listening* to your family member's perspective.

Chapter 5

Healing through Acceptance

Accept one another, then, just as Christ accepted you.

Romans 15:7 NIV

Sometimes my hypocrisy is laughable. Here is a pattern that has repeated itself in my parenting. I will look one of my children in the eyes, and with a genuine spirit I will say, "I do not expect you to be perfect. I expect you to make mistakes." Then, later that day, when they do something wrong, I get angry and say, "I *can't believe* you just did that!" The reality is that while I tell my children, and tell myself, that I don't expect them to be perfect, in some ways I do. That is part of the reason why I am shocked or surprised when they behave badly. Expecting perfection is a surefire path to broken family relationships, while accepting each other's frailties and brokenness is a path to peace.

The Acceptance of God

You have probably heard many times over the course of your life that God loves you. It is true! But did you know that God

67

also *accepts* you? Through the sacrifice of His Son, all of your sins have been covered, paid for, and forgiven. You are accepted, adopted, and wanted. Now don't miss this! God continues to accept you even though you continue to sin and fall short of His glory. God's love for you, and His acceptance of you, does not rise and fall based on your performance. Nor did you build yourself up to a certain level of holiness before God worked in your life and brought you into a relationship with Him. Here is a mind-blowing Scripture from Romans 5:8: "*But God shows*

> God's love for you, and His
> acceptance of you, does not rise
> and fall based on your performance.

his love for us in that while we were still sinners, Christ died for us." God extended His love while we were His enemies! "*In this is love, not that we have loved God but that he loved us and sent his Son to be the propitiation for our sins*" (1 John 4:10).

Take a short pause here. If this doesn't sink into your spirit, the rest of the chapter will not be helpful to you. Consider speaking these words out loud: "My heavenly Father loves me. My heavenly Father accepts me in Christ. He will always accept me. He is not shocked when I sin and fall short. He won't be shocked when I sin and fall short tomorrow. His love for me is constant, even when my love for Him is not."

Those Who Have Been Forgiven Much Love Much

Jesus was having dinner in a Pharisee's house. A "sinful" woman entered and washed Jesus' feet with her tears. The Pharisees were appalled that Jesus would allow such a woman to minister to Him in this fashion. Jesus then confronted His host by pointing out the woman's love for Him through her kindness. He said, "*Therefore I tell you, her sins, which are many, are forgiven—for she loved much. But he who is forgiven little, loves little*" (Luke 7:47). Jesus said those who have been forgiven much love much. In the same way, when we truly experience God's acceptance in light of our sins, we are able to accept others, in light of their sins. At the end of the day today, after the sins I will likely commit, Jesus will still accept me. Will I follow the example of Jesus when it comes to my family members? At the end of today, after the sins they will likely commit, will I still accept them?

God's acceptance of us is infinitely more radical and complete than our acceptance of others. God knows everything about me. He knows my secret thoughts. He sees my secret deeds. He discerns even the motives behind my "noble" actions. With His full-and-complete knowledge of my whole person, He loves me and accepts me in Christ. Imagine if your family knew *everything* about you. Imagine if all your thoughts were broadcasted on a TV screen above your head. Imagine if everything you muttered under your breath in private was spoken face-to-face. Your family members would likely be appalled, and forgiveness, acceptance, and understanding would be a long way off. When we rightly see the greatness of our sin, and the greatness of God's acceptance, we are then in a proper position to humbly accept the other sinners in our family.

Jesus Is Not Ashamed of You

Some of us were wounded by parents who told us they were ashamed of us. Perhaps you grew up in a home where you always felt like you were falling short of expectations. Did you know that if you have repented of your sins and trusted Jesus, He is not ashamed to call you His brother (Hebrews 2:11)? I grew up with an older brother, and I remember an incident when he had a group of friends over. Of course, I wanted to be a "cool big kid" and get in on the action. He would have nothing to do with it and told me to go play with my little friends. While he had every right to have times with just his buddies, at the time I felt he was ashamed of me.

Consider the power of this principle from Hebrews 2. Imagine there is a room full of people, and Jesus is there. You walk into the room. Jesus sees you and loudly says, "Hi! Come over here. Hey, everyone, I want you to meet my brother." He is not ashamed to call us His brother or sister. He *accepts* you.

Acceptance and Hope

The apostle Paul demonstrated this powerful principle of acceptance in his spiritual care for the Christians at the church in Corinth. This church, this spiritual family, was a mess. They were suing each other. They were divided over their favorite pastors. Sexual sin was being ignored, and they were getting drunk during the communion meal. It was not a pretty picture. Paul needed to write to them. He was their pastor and brother in Christ. Here was how he started his second letter: "*Our hope for you is unshaken*" (2 Corinthians 1:7).

I don't think I would have started my letter like that. How could Paul talk about hope in light of the condition of the church? Paul wrote from a spirit of love and acceptance. Parents, we need God to give us this spirit toward our children. Let our hope for them be unshaken! I am not talking about having "hope in hope," but of having hope in Jesus, who promises to never leave us or forsake us. Paul's hope for his brothers and sisters in Corinth was not naïve or passive. He directly confronted them at every point where it was needed. Yet his entire letter was wrapped in acceptance and hope.

Messed-Up People Accept Messed-Up People

The mind-set here is not, *I have it all together, but I need to be gracious and accept my messed-up family members.* How quickly and easily pride fills our hearts! Instead, we begin with an honest assessment of our own chronic and ongoing character problems, and from that point of humility we ask the Lord to help us accept our family members with all *their* baggage.

There is a *"do to others as you would have them do to you"* principle here (Luke 6:31 NIV). I know that when I mess up and offend someone in my family, I expect that they will be gracious and forgiving. I want them to cut me some slack, understand that I am under a lot of stress, or know that I wasn't trying to be rude. In other words, I want them to forgive me quickly, overlook my offense, and move on without harboring bitterness toward me. We all want this kind of gracious response from our family members. Fair enough. But are we committed to providing this kind of response to our siblings when they hurt us? We demand consideration and tolerance but are often slow to give consideration and tolerance to others.

If we view ourselves as mature and healthy but see our family members as "messed up," then it is easy for us to demand acceptance and forgiveness from them when we make mistakes. It may well be that you *are* more mature and relationally healthy than others in your family. If that is the case, that is not a warrant for pride, but you have a greater responsibility to exercise humility as you seek peace and healing in your family relationships.

Accepting the Baggage

Every one of your family members comes with baggage. Baggage goes by many names—issues, problems, dysfunctions, unhealthy patterns, wounds, sins, etc. Every one of my family

71

members is chock-full of these, and I am too. Part of choosing to be in relationship with someone is choosing to accept their baggage. This does not mean we don't confront hurtful behavior or set up necessary boundaries, but simply that your father's baggage comes with him. If you want him in your life, the baggage is part of the deal.

Earlier, I shared with you about my journey with my father. After my parents' divorce, as I was struggling with bitterness and anger toward him, I desperately wanted him to acknowledge his infidelity. I wanted a confession and an apology. But years went by, and these things never came. He was unrepentant. In fact, it was worse than that. In the years after their divorce, my father dated and lived with other women, none of whom he

> Every one of your family members
> comes with baggage.

married. There was a pattern in those years of his prioritizing these women ahead of his family. So not only did I have the wounds of the past, but also the fresh wounds of the present.

My father was not a Christian, and he was living like someone who was spiritually dead and far from God. He had lots of baggage. As the Lord brought me through the phases of forgiveness, He also brought me to a place of acceptance. I had a choice to make. I could either have no relationship with my father, or I could choose to have a relationship with my father *and* his baggage. With God's help, I chose the latter. I chose to accept the fact that my father had an area of chronic deep brokenness and dysfunction. It wasn't easy. His ongoing choices and behavior were hurtful to me, and I was continually revisiting the forgiveness process so that anger and bitterness would not take root in my heart.

72

You may be facing a similar choice with your family member. There is a fork in the road. You can choose the path of having no relationship or a severely limited relationship. (When relationships are particularly toxic or abusive, this path may be necessary, and we will explore this further in chapter 7, "Healing through Boundaries.") The other choice is the path of acceptance. You can choose to *accept* your family member with his or her baggage. You may choose this path for the sake of love. You love your husband, so you are willing to carry the extra weight of his baggage as part of what it means to be in relationship with him. You love your daughter, so you choose to accept her *with* all her selfishness and her pattern of poor decisions. This is how our heavenly Father continues to love His children, *with* all our sins and struggles—past, present, and future.

While you might think this kind of acceptance is radical, it is nothing more than the kind of acceptance we hope (and expect) to *receive* from our family members. If we are always late, we expect our family members to tolerate, understand,

> Family relationships are on the way to healing when acceptance is a two-way street.

and accept that about us. If we are absent-minded and lose track of details, we want our family to graciously accept that as just "who we are" and not get bent out of shape about it. Even in cases where we have done deeply hurtful things to others in our home, we desire genuine forgiveness. Family relationships are on the way to healing when acceptance is a two-way street.

Acceptance Is Not . . .

Acceptance is not blind. When we choose to accept a family member *with* their baggage, it doesn't mean that we pretend the baggage doesn't exist. It is a choice of love. When God accepts us, He does not turn a blind eye to our sin. Instead, He deals with it head on through the death of Christ on the cross, and He calls us to confession and repentance. Accepting your son does not mean turning a blind eye to his selfishness. Accepting him does not mean pretending that his pattern of critical, biting words doesn't exist. In fact, true acceptance is a removal of any rose-colored glasses. It is more honest. It is more real. Acceptance is a wide-eyed, wise, intentional, and honest assessment of your son's issues, while at the same time choosing to be in a relationship with him and understanding that those issues are going to be present.

Acceptance is not approval. I made the choice to accept a relationship with my father, knowing that accepting this relationship meant dealing with an ongoing pattern of my dad having unhealthy relationships with women. Accepting him with his struggles was never an affirmation or approval of his behavior. His choices hurt me. It required continual spiritual work to forgive him.

In some circumstances, other family members may not understand your choice to accept someone else's baggage. "How can you continue to have a relationship with them? Why do you keep putting up with all that junk?" They are free to make their own choices and set up their own boundaries. In these circumstances, you may need to explain to other family members that your choice of acceptance is not the same as approval.

Acceptance is not silent. There were times I needed to share my hurt feelings with my father when he prioritized his dating relationships over our family relationships. Once I became an adult, I was only able to see my father about once a year, since we lived halfway across the country from each other. When I was able to make the trip out east, it was important to me to see my dad. I remember his missing a family gathering because his girlfriend had a family event at the same time. The Lord helped me have an honest conversation with him in which I told him how his choice had hurt me. It did not go well. He did not understand my perspective or how his choice to be with his girlfriend (instead of me) had affected me. But it was important *for me* to tell him how I felt. It was healing for me, even if the conversation was, on its surface, unproductive.

I have an incredible wife. Amy truly accepts me, warts and all. But her acceptance of me does not mean she is perpetually silent. When her feelings get hurt, she lets me know. When there are character issues in my life, she lovingly seeks to help me grow. Her love for me covers a multitude of sins, yet her love for me also drives her to challenge me.

Acceptance is not prayerless. When the Lord gives us the grace to accept the realities of a broken relationship, there is peace, but there is also sadness. We want more. We want more than functional, cordial, and tolerable relationships in our homes. When we choose to accept a present and authentic relationship with our family member, it doesn't mean we want the status quo to continue. We are choosing acceptance because we are seeking healing, reconciliation, and transformation. Therefore, acceptance and prayer go together—we accept our family member with all their baggage while praying for God to bring transformation to the relationship.

Questions for Reflection and Discussion

1. God fully accepts you in and through Christ. What about that statement impacts you the most?

2. Do you struggle with expecting your family members to be perfect? Are you shocked when they sin? Why?

3. Is there someone in your life who truly accepts you? What impact has that person's love and acceptance for you had in your life?

4. Think of a family member who has extra baggage. What would it look like for you to make a choice to accept him or her *with* their baggage? How might that choice positively affect your relationship?

Chapter 6

Healing through Spiritual Warfare

For we do not wrestle against flesh and blood, but against the rulers, against the authorities, against the cosmic powers over this present darkness, against the spiritual forces of evil in the heavenly places.

Ephesians 6:12

I love coaching Little League baseball. Have you ever watched a group of six-year-olds play a game of T-ball? The kids are out there in the field. The parents are in the stands. The game is happening, but the outfielders are staring at the plane flying overhead, the shortstop is sitting in the dirt playing with ants, and the first baseman is focused on chewing his mitt. Most of the coaching at this level is in shouting, "Keep your eye on the ball! Pay attention! Get ready!"

This is how many Christians go through life. We are out there on the field, but we are not paying attention to the real-and-present battle going on around us—specifically when it comes to the reality of Satan and his demons. When we are in a conflict with a family member, it is easy to see him or her as the problem or even our "enemy." But God reminds us in the Scripture above that "we do not wrestle against flesh and blood, but against the spiritual forces of evil." It may be true that we have a significant conflict with our spouse in the *seen* world, but we are in a far more significant conflict with the demons in the *unseen* world.

Demons Strike the Base

In the beginning, God created the family as the foundation of human life. Manhood, womanhood, marriage, and family form the essential base for churches, communities, and nations. Satan and his demons focus their power and strategies to hurt the people of God and stop the advance of the gospel. How do they do this? Much of their spiritual firepower is directed at God's institution of the family. This is one reason why family relationships are so difficult and conflictual. The demons want to divide your family and are working to make it happen.

> God created the family as the
> foundation of human life.

While we may experience demonic temptation and deception at work, I believe they will direct more of their evil strategies against us at home. They are going to seek to shatter your relationships with your siblings more than your relationships with your neighbors. The demons hate what God loves. God loves your family. He intentionally brought you into the world with these specific people as a part of your family. It is His desire to use your family as a light for Christ in the world and for future generations. Because God so loves and has a divine plan for your family, Satan and the demons hate it. They are actively working to sow hatred, discord, violence, anger, resentment, adultery, jealousy, and every other sin deep into your family tree.

Jesus tells us in John 10:10 about the work of Satan, "*The thief comes only to steal and kill and destroy.*" The apostle Peter warns us in 1 Peter 5:8, "*Be sober-minded; be watchful. Your adversary the devil prowls about like a roaring lion, seeking someone to devour.*" Our families are in the middle of an all-out spiritual war! We have spiritual enemies who are active, engaged, and on the attack. The demons would love nothing more than for us to ignore this battle. They do not want to face any resistance to their plans. But God calls us not only to be aware of the spiritual battle raging around us, but also to engage in it. "*Therefore take up the whole armor of God, that you may be able to withstand in the evil day, and having done all, to stand firm*" (Ephesians 6:13).

Seeking Peace through Fighting

It seems counterintuitive that we should seek peace by fighting, but there are times when that is exactly what we need to do. We need to stop fighting against our family and start fighting against the spiritual forces of evil. There may be some Christians who place too much emphasis on the activity of demons, seeing evil spirits under every rock and behind every door. However, I think most believers today are at the opposite end of the spectrum, paying far too little or even no attention to how demonic spirits may be at work in their lives and family relationships.

Before we talk about the specific ways we can engage in this spiritual battle, we need to affirm some spiritual realities. First,

Satan and God are not coequal powers in the universe. In the movies, there is the "good side" and the "dark side," and we have to wait until the dramatic conclusion to see who will win. The real world is not like that. God is the supreme, all-powerful Creator of the universe. Satan is a fallen creature. Satan and

> We need to stop fighting against our family and start fighting against the spiritual forces of evil.

his demons are allowed to do only what God permits. Jesus came into the world *"to destroy the works of the devil"* (1 John 3:8), and He did this through His coming, His sinless life, His death, His resurrection, and ultimately His return. At the Last Judgment, Satan and all his demons will be thrown into hell forever.

It is because of Christ's complete victory over the evil spirits that we can confidently engage in this spiritual battle. Consider God's instruction to us found in James 4:7: *"Submit yourselves therefore to God. Resist the devil, and he will flee from you."* Because the Spirit of the living Christ dwells in our hearts, we have spiritual authority over the demons. It is because Jesus dwells in the heart of the believer that a Christian cannot be possessed by a demon. The Christian is already "possessed" by Christ. There is no vacancy for an evil spirit. However, a born-again Christian can be influenced, tempted, attacked, and oppressed by demons. God warns believers in Ephesians 4:27, *"Give no opportunity to the devil."* Other translations say, *"Neither give place to the devil"* (KJV) and *"Do not give the devil a foothold"* (NIV). As believers, we must be on our guard, because we have spiritual enemies who are both real and powerful. If we are careless, we can give these evil spirits opportunities, space, and footholds to attack us and our families. Let's walk through four spiritual battle strategies that we can use to pursue peace and healing in our family relationships.

Fight against Demonic Temptation

If Christ himself was tempted by a demon (Satan himself), we can expect to be tempted as well. But we are not defenseless against demonic temptation. *"For because he himself has suffered when tempted, he is able to help those who are being tempted"* (Hebrews 2:18). There are two demonic temptations that are common in family conflicts: the temptation to hold on to a spirit of anger, and the temptation to take vengeance.

Temptation toward anger

In a previous chapter, we explored the essential ingredients of forgiveness. Part of forgiving is being set free from a spirit of anger. Therefore, the demons will tempt us to hold on to an attitude of anger to prevent true forgiveness from taking place. The demons tempt us to hold on to anger because they know that *"the anger of man does not produce the righteousness of God"* (James 1:20). Consider using this spiritual battle prayer to fight back against any demonic temptation seeking to fill your heart with anger toward your family member.

> *Lord, I thank you for your victory over the devil and his demons. I thank you that you endured all of Satan's temptations and that you have given me your promise that you will enable me to endure every evil temptation as well. In the name of Jesus I come against any evil spirit who would tempt me to hold on to a heart of anger toward _____ [name of your family member]. My anger will never produce your righteousness. I reject this temptation*

81

*to be angry and bitter. Take away any anger or hatred I
have in my heart toward _____ and replace it with
a spirit of love and compassion.*

Temptation toward vengeance

Vengeance may seem like a strong word, but when we are
hurt we can be easily tempted to strike back. The demons are
not content to simply tempt us to hold on to a spirit of anger.
They want that anger to foment into action. Consider God's
words from Ephesians 4:31: "*Let all bitterness and wrath and
anger and clamor and slander be put away from you, along with
all malice.*" Take a close look at the list. Bitterness, wrath, and
anger are sins of the heart, which can then overflow into fighting
(clamor) and slander. The demons will tempt us to *take action*
on our anger. Often we feel quite justified in this. Considering
everything this person has done to hurt you, they have it coming, right? It may be that justice needs to be served, but that is
God's department, not ours. "*Beloved, never avenge yourselves,
but leave it to the wrath of God, for it is written, 'Vengeance is
mine, I will repay, says the Lord'*" (Romans 12:19).

Perhaps your family member has hurt you through his coldness and withdrawal. Demons may tempt you to return the same
coldness. You may be tempted to give him the silent treatment
or just be "politely" disengaged for days, weeks, or months at
a time.[1] The demons may tempt you to believe that you are just
being self-protective when in fact you're being spiteful. Mirror-
ing the wrong behavior of your brother will only make things
worse! Consider this battle prayer against this demonic attack:

*Lord, I am being tempted to act on my hurt and anger
toward _____. I am being tempted to hurt _____
by withdrawing, being callous, and checking out of the
relationship. I know that is not your heart toward me*

when I hurt you through my sin. I want your heart toward
_____. In the name of Jesus I reject this demonic
temptation to take vengeance on _____. Lord, I ask
you to remove all anger and bitterness from my heart and
replace them with your love and compassion.

Sometimes the temptation to strike back at our family members is more extreme. Years ago, I was counseling a couple through their marriage crisis. She had been unfaithful. In his anger and hurt, he went out and did the same. It was not primarily because he wanted to have an affair. He wanted to hurt her just as he had been hurt. The demons had a great victory. This is not to say the demons made him do it. When we consider demonic temptation, we should not lose sight of James 1:14: *"But each person is tempted when he is lured and enticed by his own desire."*

You may be tempted to seek "an eye for an eye" with your family member. We experience this temptation from childhood. "He hit me, so I hit him back." "She broke my toy, so I broke hers." You may be many years removed from childhood, but this "eye for an eye" temptation is just as powerful in our lives today. Are you being tempted to return evil for evil with your brother or sister? Consider this spiritual battle prayer:

Lord, I confess I am being tempted to act on my anger and
hurt toward _____. Specifically, I am being tempted
to _____ in order to hurt them. In the name of
Jesus I come against this demonic temptation to take ven-
geance. I claim the truth of your Word that vengeance
belongs to you and not to me. I reject this temptation to
act on my anger. Thank you for your victory over the devil
and his demons and that you share that victory with me.

Vengeance can also take the form of slander or gossip. When we are in conflict with a family member, we naturally seek allies. We want people to hear the story of how right we are, how wrong they are, and how we deserve compassion and justice. Therefore, we are vulnerable to the temptation to talk negatively about our brother with as many people as will listen. In this moment, we may also deceive ourselves that our unloading all this negative information about our brother is for his good, or for the good of the family, or perhaps we are just "sharing a prayer need." This is not to say that it is always wrong or inappropriate to bring a friend or other family member into a conflict. We will address those situations in the pages ahead. For now, we are focusing on those all-too-familiar situations where we find ourselves speaking negatively to others about our brother, and those words are coming from a spirit of anger and payback. Are you being tempted to spread gossip or slander about someone in your family? Fight that temptation in prayer.

Lord, I am being tempted to speak negatively about _____. I know that Jesus was tempted in every way as I am, yet He did not sin. I choose to live in the power of Jesus right now. I reject and resist, in the name of Jesus, any demonic temptation to gossip or slander against _____. I ask that you fill my heart, my mind, and my mouth with words that build up others and honor you.

Fight against Demonic Deception

In John 8:44, Jesus describes Satan with the words, "*When he lies, he speaks his native language, for he is a liar and the father of lies*" (NIV). My native language is English. I know bits and pieces of other languages, but my "built-in" language is English. The built-in language of Satan is *lies*. When demons attack us in the spiritual realm, they do so through lies and deception. They want you to believe that true things are false and false things are true. In Ephesians 6, the first piece of armor we are told to put on is *the belt of truth.*

Christians are not exempt from experiencing demonic activity. I remember a time when Amy and I were caught up in an emotional conflict. Both of us were feeling hurt and distant from each other. With God's help, one of the things we try to say to each other in such moments is, "I love you, and I am committed to you." Our feelings may not be warm and fuzzy in the moment, but we choose to affirm allegiance to each other. Amy put this into practice. After our conflict, she said, "I love you, and I am committed to you." Instantly I had the thought, *That is not true. She doesn't love you. She is not committed to you.* I am sure this was a spiritual attack. I *know* Amy is committed to me. Everything in her life with me has demonstrated that truth. But a demon, knowing I was weak and hurting, tried to press this deception into my mind and heart.

There are many deceptions that can come against us when we are locked in a conflict with a family member. Here are some common ones:

- This situation is hopeless. Nothing will ever change.
- Forgiveness is not possible for you—not from God or your family.
- You would be happier with someone else. You just married the wrong person.
- The other families at your church don't have these kinds of problems.
- Your family doesn't love you.
- You should not talk about these issues with anyone else, because they would never understand and it would just make things worse.

If you find these kinds of thoughts rolling over and over in your mind, it may be due to an ongoing spiritual attack. Spiritual attacks must be met with spiritual warfare. Here is the basic prayer pattern for fighting back against spiritual lies: (1) Name the deception; (2) call it a lie; (3) reject the lie in the name of Jesus; and (4) replace the lie with God's truth.

> *Lord, I have been believing that this situation with my mother is hopeless. That is a lie. I reject that lie in the name of Jesus. Instead, I choose to believe the truth that you are the God of hope and that by the power of the Holy Spirit I will abound in hope (Romans 15:13). Because of your power and love, there is no such thing as a hopeless situation.*
>
> *God, I have been believing that forgiveness is not possible for me because of all the terrible things I have done. That is a lie. I reject that lie in the name of Jesus. I choose to believe the truth that if I confess my sins, you are faithful and just to forgive me of my sins and cleanse me from all unrighteousness (1 John 1:9).*
>
> *Lord, I have been believing that I should not talk about my burdens and concerns with others. That is a lie. I reject that lie in the name of Jesus. I replace that lie with the truth that you have put godly people in my life to help bear my burdens (Galatians 6:2) and that I can seek help from them.*

Whatever you do, don't allow your mind to repeat lies over and over in your thoughts. *I am worthless. My marriage is hopeless. No one loves me. There is no point in trying. . . .* These thoughts are *not* from God. They need to be identified as lies, and then you need to do battle against them in the spiritual realm.

Fight for Freedom

Jesus brings freedom. Satan and his demons bring bondage. *"For freedom Christ has set us free; stand firm therefore, and do not submit again to a yoke of slavery"* (Galatians 5:1).

Perhaps there is an addiction, in your life or theirs, that is playing a central role in your family conflict. While the roots of addiction are complex, they carry a spiritual component that must be addressed in the spiritual realm. Through our years in ministry, Amy and I have walked with people through the highs and lows of recovery. Breaking free from an addiction usually requires intervention, counseling, and accountability, as well as radical lifestyle choices. However, if the underlying spiritual bondage is not dealt with and broken, the addiction (or a replacement behavior just as destructive) is likely to return.

Praying against generational patterns

We see spiritual bondage not only in individuals but also in the generations of a family. Demons seek to replicate sinful patterns through the family tree, passing damage and destruction from one generation to the next. This is one reason why we see violence, addiction, anger, and many other sins spread through families. But there is good news! Because of Christ's resurrection from the dead, we are not doomed to carry on the sinful and hurtful patterns of our families. Our generation, and the future generations that come from us, do not need to continue to live in bondage.

As I shared earlier, my mother was the first Christian in our family tree. The Lord brought her to faith in Jesus when I was a baby. She later led my brother and me to the Lord, so we became the first Christian men in our recent family tree. As we looked around, we recognized that one of the primary attacks the enemy had waged against our family was in destroying

87

marriages. My father had been divorced three times before he married my mother. My mother had been divorced once. There were other divorces and broken marriages in my extended family. This was a toxic pattern. Seeing the pattern, my mother encouraged my brother and me to fight against this generational curse in the spiritual realm. She helped us to put in practice a rarely used biblical prayer strategy called *representative repentance.*

We find examples of representative repentance numerous times in the Bible. The prophet Jeremiah repented to God as a *representative* of the people of Israel: "*Although our sins testify against us, O Lord, do something for the sake of your name. For our backsliding is great; we have sinned against you*" (Jeremiah 14:7 NIV1984). He confessed and sought forgiveness, not just for himself but also for his spiritual family.

Daniel exemplified this spiritual practice as well. He believed that God would restore the people of Israel to the Promised Land, so he sought God in prayer. Daniel prayed and confessed, "*O Lord, the great and awesome God, who keeps his covenant of love with all who love him and obey his commands, we have sinned and done wrong. We have been wicked and have rebelled; we have turned away from your commands and laws*" (Daniel 9:4–5 NIV1984).

These men came before God in prayer and confessed the sins of their people. They came as representatives of a larger group, repenting of the sins of the entire group to the Lord. In many of these cases, the individual praying was not guilty of the sin being confessed. Did Daniel turn away from God and reject the Scriptures? Absolutely not! Nevertheless, Daniel, as a representative of the people of Israel, humbled himself and confessed, seeking the mercy of God.

My mother led my brother and me to follow this prayer pattern, waging war against our generational pattern of unbiblical divorce.

*Lord, we come to you as representatives of our family.
We are here to confess to you the pattern of unbiblical
divorce in our family tree. We repent of this. We ask that
you would apply the cross of Christ to the generations
of our family and set us free from this sinful pattern. We
pray against and reject, in the name of Jesus, any demonic
attack against our marriages and the future marriages of
our children. Please end this pattern in our generation,
and in the generations to come.*

Take a moment and consider the unhealthy patterns in your family tree. You may need to explore this with a trusted Christian friend or your pastor. When we look at the families in the Bible, we find all kinds of generational patterns, including favoritism, laziness, abuse, arrogance, greed, anger, and involvement with false religions. What patterns do you see in your family? You may want to write down your thoughts in a journal and, after identifying some of these generational patterns, do spiritual battle against them by practicing representative repentance.

Don't Just Talk about Fighting

While it would be wrong to blame demonic forces for all our problems, it would be equally foolish to ignore the reality that a spiritual battle is being waged against our souls and family relationships. Many Christians would say, "I think demons are real and that they are at work against us." It is one thing to acknowledge that we are in a spiritual battle and an entirely different thing to engage in that battle. This is an action book, and this is an action chapter. I don't want your eyes to simply be opened to the spiritual battle around you. I want you to engage in it through prayer, with the Word of God, and in the authority of Jesus Christ. The prayer examples in this chapter will help get you started.

Amy and I were talking about the spiritual battles we were facing in our family relationships when she shared with me a picture the Lord had brought to her mind while she was at Starbucks. She imagined being in the middle of a battlefield while sitting at a nice little table, sipping her coffee. The Lord was encouraging her that it was not enough for her to acknowledge that there was warfare taking place in our family relationships. She needed to do something about it through active prayer.

This may be a good time to stop reading. Take a few moments and write out some "battle Scriptures" and "warfare prayers," then post them on your bathroom mirror, phone background, or screen saver. It's time to stop giving the devil a foothold in our homes and family relationships. It may seem as though your family is the enemy right now, but the spiritual forces of evil in the heavenly realms are a far more sinister enemy. If we want more peace in our homes, we need to do more fighting.

Questions for Reflection and Discussion

1. How much attention have you paid to these issues of spiritual warfare in your personal life and in your family relationships?
2. In your church family, or among your friends, do you think there is too much or too little attention given to spiritual warfare?
3. In what ways are you tempted to sin and make things worse with your family relationships? Identify that temptation and use the prayer patterns from this chapter to wage war against it.

4. Ask the Lord to reveal to you any deceptions that have taken root in your mind regarding your relationship with God or your family. Use the prayer pattern above to fight back against those lies.

5. Engaging in spiritual battle prayers can feel overwhelming or even scary. Is there a trusted Christian friend, counselor, or pastor who would be willing to meet with you to talk through the principles and prayers in this chapter?

Chapter 7

Healing through Boundaries

A man of great wrath will pay the penalty, for if you deliver him, you will only have to do it again.

Proverbs 19:19

When I think of seeking healing in a relationship, I think of words like *kindness*, *forgiveness*, and *acceptance*. However, sometimes the biblical thing to do—the healing thing to do—is to establish healthy boundaries, to say no, and to step out of a toxic system. There is nothing "Christian" or "spiritual" about allowing ourselves to be mistreated, railroaded, or disrespected within the context of a family relationship.[1] This is a difficult chapter for me to write. I am a rescuer. I want everyone happy all the time, and I feel responsible for their feelings. I say yes at times when I should say no. Sometimes I am not honest with my feelings in order to avoid conflict. These are all examples of poor boundaries, patterns that result in short-term peace but long-term problems. My choices might seem to help in the heat of the moment, yet I hurt myself and the relationships within my family in the long run.

Here is a small example. I remember a situation when I was facing a deadline with a project for work. Before I left the house in the morning, I went over the day's schedule, including my work commitments, with Amy. A little before lunch, Amy texted me and asked if I would be able to pick up some groceries on the way home. My stress was already high, and I was annoyed that she was asking me to run this errand. I quickly replied, "Yes. No problem." I wanted to help her, but it was a mistake. Later that afternoon, I wrapped up my work, rushed to the store, and hustled home. I came into the house on edge, and my negative emotions affected the rest of the evening. Amy had done nothing wrong by asking me to run an errand. The conflictual evening was not her fault. If I had been wiser, I would have kindly told her that I wanted to help, but that with my work commitments that day it was not possible. That would have been a healthy boundary that would have led to more peace in our home.

To better understand what boundaries are and how they work, let's consider two examples from Scripture: first, the story of Joseph and his brothers, and second, a conflict that took place in Jesus' family.

Joseph Set a Boundary with His Brothers

Earlier in the book, we looked at the miraculous account of Joseph's reconciliation with his brothers. Let's examine this again with an eye toward understanding the principle of boundary setting. When the ten brothers first appeared before Joseph, asking for food, Joseph recognized them. Why did he not reveal his identity to them at that time? Why not commence with the family reunion? Joseph seems to have set for himself a clear, personal boundary. He had been violently abused by his brothers and sold into slavery. Before he would open his heart to them, he needed to see two things. First, Joseph wanted to see if the brothers had taken responsibility for what they had done to him. Would there be any sense of godly sorrow and repentance? Second, he needed to see that they had changed their ways. Were they still abusers? Were they still selfish and violent? He would not offer his trust to them if the brothers were unchanged.

In Genesis 42:21, Joseph overhears the brothers admitting what they did to him, acknowledging their guilt and even expressing their awareness that they deserve justice. When he hears this, Joseph weeps. But words were not enough for Joseph. He still would not reveal himself to them. Later, in Genesis 44:33, Judah offers his own life for Benjamin out of love for his little brother and love for his father. Years ago, it was Judah who had suggested that Joseph be sold into slavery (Genesis 37:26–27), and now he is willing to become a slave to save Benjamin.

It was only after Joseph heard the brothers express their guilt and sorrow, and saw them demonstrate a change in their behavior, that he lowered his *boundary* and revealed his identity to them. We then see true healing and reconciliation in their relationships and family. Yet this reconciliation would not have been possible (or healthy) without Joseph's boundaries.

Imagine if Joseph, upon seeing the brothers for the first time in Egypt, had hugged them and invited them all to live with him in Egypt? Imagine if he had told them, "Let's forget everything and never talk about it." That would have been an option, but it would not have been *reconciliation*. It would have been sweeping the abuse under the rug, leaving the wounds of the past to fester, and would have prevented genuine trust from forming in the future.

Jesus Set a Boundary with His Family

In Mark 3, Jesus' public ministry was now in full swing. His family did not yet fully understand who Jesus was, or the mis-

sion that He had been sent to accomplish. Jesus had been healing the sick, casting out demons, forgiving sins, and confronting
the Pharisees. His family thought that Jesus was "out of his
mind" (Mark 3:21), and they went out to "seize him" and bring
Him back home.

> And his mother and his brothers came, and standing outside
> they sent to him and called him. And a crowd was sitting around
> him, and they said to him, "Your mother and your brothers are
> outside, seeking you." And he answered them, "Who are my
> mother and my brothers?" And looking about at those who sat
> around him, he said, "Here are my mother and my brothers!
> For whoever does the will of God, he is my brother and sister
> and mother."
>
> Mark 3:31–35

Jesus said no to His family. While Scripture does not tell
us specifically, I think it would be fair to assume that Jesus'
mother and brothers were not pleased. He made a choice and
set a boundary, knowing His family might be upset. Why would
Jesus do this? He loved His family. He honored His mother. He
set a boundary because in this situation His family was seeking
to prevent Him from obeying His heavenly Father. His family,
even with their good intentions, was, in this moment, spiritually toxic to Him. Jesus chose to please God rather than man.

Boundaries with Unbelieving Family Members

Many Christians today face this same challenge. Perhaps your
spouse is not a believer and does not want you to attend church.
What should you do? Some have told me, "I want to show love
and support for my spouse. I need to put my marriage first
and honor his request. I don't want him to be angry with me."

While it may be true that stopping your participation in church will placate your spouse, it will not in any way create more love and oneness in your marriage. In fact, two serious consequences will likely come from this failed boundary. First, your spouse has succeeded in their inappropriate attempt to control *your* spiritual life and choices. With that success, he or she will likely seek to exert more control in additional areas of your life. Second, and more important, you have made the choice to please your spouse rather than please God. If you are in a "spiritually single" marriage, you need your church family more than ever before. In the end, your marriage and your own heart will be worse off if you fail to establish a healthy boundary.

Perhaps you are one of the first Christians in your family tree. God has put a special calling on your life. He may call you to lead a spiritual transformation that will ripple forward for generations to come. However, you may face some lonely and difficult waters. My friend Mike found himself in this situation. He is the only Christian among his siblings, and the family was making plans for his younger brother's wedding. His brother asked him to be his best man, and he was honored to accept.

> When we set healthy boundaries,
> there may be short-term pain,
> but we create an opportunity
> for long-term gain.

However, the groom-to-be planned a multiday bachelor-party trip, filled with many inappropriate activities, prior to the wedding day. Mike knew that saying no to the bachelor-party trip would not only offend his brother but also his other siblings and his parents. But he also knew that to go on the trip and participate in ungodly activities would dishonor God and his wife. He informed his brother that he would be able to join the group on the first day of the trip (prior to the start of the sleazy stuff), but that he would need to fly home early and skip the last two days. He set a boundary. His brother and the rest of the family did not understand. They felt hurt and rejected, and perhaps behind his back they accused him of being a "Jesus freak." But by setting this healthy boundary, Mike honored God, honored his wife, and was authentic in his relationship with his brother. He did not try to control his brother's choices, and at the same time he did not allow his brother to control his. When we set healthy boundaries, there may be short-term pain, but we create an opportunity for long-term gain.

A Difficult Teaching from Jesus

We are to eagerly seek healing and oneness in our family relationships. That is the whole focus of this book. However, there are no guarantees that our family relationships will heal. Jesus speaks this truth to us in Luke 12. You will rarely hear a pastor preach on this passage. There is nothing warm or fuzzy about it. Consider these words of Jesus:

> "Do you think that I have come to give peace on earth? No, I tell you, but rather division. For from now on in one house there will be five divided, three against two and two against three. They will be divided, father against son and son against father, mother against daughter and daughter against mother, mother-in-law against her daughter-in-law and daughter-in-law against mother-in-law."
>
> Luke 12:51–53

How do we reconcile this passage with Jesus bringing peace on earth and goodwill toward men? In this teaching, Jesus is simply giving us unvarnished truth. The reality is that when some members of a family repent and follow Jesus, while others reject Him, there will be spiritual division in that family. I expand on this in my book *Limited Church*:

> In the first century, it was a life-threatening decision to worship Jesus. From the Roman perspective, worshipping Jesus as a god was no problem. There were many gods. Take your pick. But to worship Jesus *alone* as God was unacceptable. Not only would your life be in danger from the political powers, but from your parents and siblings as well. Jesus was simply speaking the truth of what was to come, that if you follow Him, your family might try to kill you (Matthew 10:21–22). Jesus' words remain true to this day. In many families and countries around the world, particularly in Muslim contexts, to trust Christ means putting one's life in jeopardy. Who would kill you for simply "changing your religion"? Your father. Your brother. In the western world, where we generally enjoy religious freedom because of our Christian heritage, it is hard for us to understand how such things could happen. This was reality for many Christians in the first century, as it is for many Christians around the world today.[2]

Setting Boundaries with Unhealthy Family Members

Steve and Karen reached out to an expert in grandparenting ministry for help with a difficult situation with Karen's parents. They were observing a pattern of her parents behaving in unhealthy ways around their two children, ages five and seven. Her father had a long-standing habit of swearing and did not hesitate to use this kind of language around the kids. Her mother had a pattern of putting herself in the position of "the mom," even to the point of undercutting Steve and Karen's parenting. She quickly took on the role of primary disciplinarian, setting up her own rules, and was unduly harsh in the process. Though Steve and Karen were concerned, they did not address the issues for many months. In their family, problems were not dealt with directly. They did not want to do anything to dishonor Karen's parents. Instead, they chose the "path of peace," hoping that things would get better over time.

They soon noticed three things beginning to happen. First, the unhealthy patterns from the grandparents were in fact getting worse. Second, the children were becoming increasingly upset, even at the mention of their going to visit the grandparents. Third, Steve and Karen were becoming angry and bitter. Something had to change. The "path of peace" was only making things worse.

Their counselor encouraged them to take a risk, to establish a boundary and directly address the issue with Karen's parents. They asked the grandparents if there was a good time for them to have a personal conversation, and this is a summary of how Steve approached the conversation:

> "Thanks for being willing to talk with us. First, we want to tell you that we love you and appreciate you. Because we care about our relationship with you and your relationship with our kids, we need to have an important conversation. Dad, I know that you use some swearwords, but those are not appropriate words to use in our house or around our children. It is not good for the kids to hear that kind of language. Mom, sometimes when you are dealing with the kids, especially when they misbehave, you are harsh with them. Also, there have been times when you know that we have a rule for something, but you ignore our rules and establish your own. This is a pattern that needs to change. We want to have a great relationship with you, and we want you to have great relationships with the kids. But if these things don't change, we won't be able to spend as much time together."

These were not easy words to speak. Steve and Karen took a big risk. They chose to break out of an unhealthy family pattern, to deal with things directly and set a boundary. This story has a happy ending. The initial conversation was awkward, and they left without a clear resolution. But over the next few weeks, Karen's parents, *who wanted to keep a relationship with their grandkids*, decided to work on making changes. And while things were not perfect, they were improved. Setting a boundary was necessary to bring healing for the generations of this family.

A Challenge with an Adult Child

Marcus was twenty-two years old. He had tried college for a year but did not have the grades or motivation to keep going, so he moved back in with his mom. Kelly had divorced from Marcus's dad eight years prior, and she knew how much the divorce had affected him. His dad was not involved in Marcus's life, so Kelly did everything she could to help him. Things were not that much different from when Marcus was in junior high. Mom cooked his meals and did his laundry. She even cleaned his room. Kelly tried to encourage him that he either needed to go back to school or get a job, but neither happened, even though she had helped to line up two job interviews for him. Instead, Marcus was spending most of his time playing video games and hanging out with friends who were similarly adrift.

Kelly became increasingly frustrated on two fronts. First, it seemed that despite all she was doing to help support Marcus, he rarely expressed any appreciation. In fact, he was often critical of her cooking! Second, she had reached a boiling point with his unwillingness to go back to school or get a job, but he seemed content to live off her modest income. At this point, most days were filled with conflict and irritation. Something had to change.

Kelly's pastor helped her to see that while her efforts to help Marcus transition into adulthood were well-intentioned, she had poor boundaries. She was doing things for Marcus that he could (and should) have been doing for himself. So even though her intent was to help, she was actually preventing Marcus from taking personal responsibility for key areas of his life. In addition, their relationship was increasingly broken. Kelly was bitter and resentful toward her son, and he was irritated and disrespectful toward his mom. In order to seek healing in the relationship, and help her son thrive, Kelly set some boundaries. It went like this:

"Marcus, I want you to know that I love you and I am committed to you. Because I love you, I need to have a difficult conversation with you. I think I have made some mistakes over these past couple of years since you came home after that first year of college.

"The bottom line is that I have not treated you like an adult. I have done things for you that I should have let you do for yourself. I have been doing your laundry and picking up after you. You know I have been on you about getting a job, but I have been the one who has been out there trying to schedule interviews for you. I now realize that while I thought I was helping by doing all those things, I was making things worse.

"This pattern has also hurt our relationship. There has been a lot more conflict between us lately, and I think some of that is because of these unwise choices I have made. So, for the sake of our relationship, I have decided to make some changes. Some are small, and others are big. First, your laundry is your laundry. Let me know if you need me to teach you how to use the machines. Second, I am no longer going to pay for gas for your car. I will keep paying for your insurance until you get a job, but the gas is up to you. Third, I have decided that if you are not back to school full-time or working full-time within six months, then you will need to find another place to live.

"You are welcome here, but it is not good for you, for me, or for our relationship for us to continue with the way things are right now. I love you, and I am committed to you. I hope we can work on these things together."

Unfortunately, Marcus was not immediately responsive to his mom's plan. Frankly, he didn't think she would follow through on her boundaries. But Kelly began to make some changes. She left his laundry in his room, and slowly he began to spend time in the laundry room. She stopped giving him cash for gas. His car sat in the driveway a lot, as he usually asked friends to pick him up if they were going out. They are approaching the six-month mark and things are up in the air. Marcus has a potential job lined up, yet he has not sealed the deal. Kelly is wavering on whether she should ask him to leave. Setting boundaries is rarely neat and tidy. The good news is that while Kelly and Marcus are working through the ups and downs of these new patterns, their relationship has improved! There is more peace and less stress in the home.

Boundary Setters Become the Bad Guys

In some family systems, hurtful behavior is swept under the rug. Relationships become damaged and frayed, with issues never getting discussed. Meanwhile, anger and coldness seethe under the surface. Unhealthy behavior is continually tolerated, and so it continues. We have seen this pattern many times in our counseling ministry. Oftentimes when one family member decides that he or she has had enough of these patterns and directly confronts the hurtful behavior, the other family members turn on them and accuse them of *causing* the problem.

Imagine your house is burning down, but no one is talking about it. Everyone is still inside and going about their business.

You shout, "The house is on fire!" To which everyone shouts back, "Shut your mouth! How could you be so mean to say such a thing about our house?" I want to give you fair warning that setting boundaries will require courage and it will stir things up, as you are no longer "playing along" with the broken family system. You are unwilling to sit silently in a house that is burning down around you. When you set boundaries, you may be accused of being unloving, but in reality you have shifted into a mode where you are *loving enough* to do something to help the family move toward healing.

Setting Boundaries on Ourselves

Sometimes we need to set boundaries with a family member. We need to say no in order to move the relationship toward healing. However, there are times when seeking reconciliation in a relationship means setting boundaries on ourselves.

I have workaholic tendencies, and this was especially true in my twenties and thirties. I struggled with setting any boundaries around my work hours. There was always one more student who needed me, one more small-group lesson to prepare, and one more leader to recruit. Not surprisingly, my lack of personal boundaries began to damage my relationship with Amy.

Here is a script that began to repeat itself. I would leave for work in the morning, and Amy would ask, "What time are you coming home tonight?"

"Hmmm. I think around five thirty."

"Great! I'll see you then."

"Okay. Love you, sweetie!"

Then around four thirty I would receive a call from a parent who was dealing with a situation with their teen and asking if I could come over to their house to help. After saying yes, I would quickly call Amy and say, "Honey, I know I said I'd be home at five thirty, but the Green family really needs my help tonight, so I probably won't be home until eight o'clock."

My wife knew what she signed up for when she married a pastor. It is not a nine-to-five job. She also understood that pastoral crises would naturally arise from time to time, so she gave her full support to me in those situations. The problem was that these "pastoral crises" were not "from time to time." They were standard operating procedure. Because of my struggle with saying no at work, I was effectively saying an even bigger no to my family.

But my poor boundaries went beyond my schedule and crazy work hours. I had unhealthy spiritual boundaries as well. As a youth pastor, my number one mission was passing my faith on to other people's children. I would pray with others' children. I would spend time with students to build discipleship relationships. I took them on retreats, mission trips, and service days. Tragically, while I was praying with other people's children, I was not praying with mine. I was teaching God's Word to other people's children, but not teaching His Word to my own. I had a purpose and a passion to lead other families to know Jesus, yet I was spiritually passive and disconnected in my home.

I also struggled with giving more consideration to congregation members than I did to my family. If someone needed to change the time of their counseling appointment with me, I would quickly agree, then call home and inform Amy that our evening plans needed to change.

In the summer of 2004, God brought me to a place of brokenness and repentance in regard to these unhealthy boundaries. The Lord convicted me that I had been putting my spiritual opportunities (my public ministry) in front of my spiritual responsibilities (my ministry to my family). I confessed and repented to Amy and our children. I committed to put them first, and one of the ways I needed to do that was by putting appropriate boundaries around my public ministry. As God helped me to say no at appropriate times at work, my family felt loved, and our marriage improved.

Billy Graham and Boundaries

I was convicted after reading Billy Graham's autobiography, *Just As I Am*. In the last chapters, he talks about some things he would have done differently:

> Ruth says those of us who were off traveling missed the best part of our lives—enjoying the children as they grew. She is probably right. I was too busy preaching all over the world. . . . I now know that I came through those years much the poorer both psychologically and emotionally. I missed so much by not being home to see the children grow and develop. The children must carry scars of those separations too. . . . I have failed many times, and I would do many things differently.
>
> For one thing, I would speak less and study more, and I would spend more time with my family. When I look back over the schedule I kept thirty or forty years ago, I am staggered by all the things we did and the engagements we kept. Sometimes we flitted from one part of the country to another, even from one continent to another, in the course of only a few days. Were all those engagements necessary? . . . Every day I was absent from my family is gone forever.[3]

Perhaps, like me, you are passionate about ministry and serving God in your church, in your community, or globally. Praise God! But our first calling, our first ministry, is to our family members.[4] I regularly pray for God to turn my heart to

Him, then to my wife, then to my children, then to my public ministry.

What Do You Need to Say No To?

Seeking healing in your family relationships may require cutting some things out of your life. Perhaps you are working on building a better relationship with your spouse, but you are struggling with porn and fantasy. One of the best things you can do, for

> Our first calling, our first ministry, is to our family members.

yourself and for your marriage, is to face up to your struggle with porn. Call your pastor or a Christian counselor. Gather trusted friends around you for accountability. Fighting the battle to say no to porn is saying a huge yes to your marriage.

Maybe the needed boundary in your life is for something less sinister. Perhaps the TV is on too much in your home, and as a result you have little to no time for conversation and building relationships with one another. Or instead of talking with each other at dinner, everyone is staring at their phones. For the sake of your family, you need new boundaries. *"Here is the time that the TV stays off." "Here is the time when our phones are away from our bodies." "Here is the time when all screens remain dark."*

If you are like me, you have a hard time setting boundaries. I don't like to say no to other people, because I want them to be happy. And I don't like saying no to myself, because I want me to be happy! Bad boundaries lead to short-term wins but long-term losses in our family relationships.

Questions for Reflection and Discussion

1. Which one of the stories in this chapter did you connect with the most? Why?

2. When was the last time you said yes to a family member when you should have said no? How did your decision affect your heart and the relationship?

3. Think about your family when you were growing up. In what ways did your family practice healthy or unhealthy boundaries?

4. Are you a rescuer like me? How do you see that pattern affecting your relationships at home?

5. Are there some habits or patterns in your life that are causing damage to your family relationships? Do you need help stopping an unhealthy behavior? Talk to God about that in prayer. Confess it to Him and ask Him who you can call to ask for their prayer, counsel, and accountability to help you grow.

Chapter 8

Healing through Compassion

When he saw the crowds, he had compassion for them, because
they were harassed and helpless, like sheep without a shepherd.

Matthew 9:36

Have you had nights of tossing and turning with anxiety? Have
you woken up with your heart racing, overwhelmed by the conflicts and hurt in your family? Consider Psalm 56:8: "*You have
kept count of my tossings; put my tears in your bottle.*" The
Lord is with you. Not one of your "tossings" escapes His attention. The second part of the verse, where David imagines the
Lord putting his tears in a bottle, is a metaphor. It is a picture
of deep compassion.

I hope you have seen a running theme in this book. Most of
the chapters begin by turning our attention to God, His love for
us, and what He has done to reconcile us to himself. Because
He forgives us, we can forgive others. Because He accepts us, we
can accept others. In this chapter, we will explore an essential
heart attitude that we need to cultivate if we want the Lord to
use us to bring healing in a family relationship. This essential
heart attitude is *compassion*.

There are many times in Scripture when God tells us of His compassion for us, and it is usually connected with our sinfulness and rebellion. Psalm 78 is a great example of this. In verses 9–37, we find a long list of Israel's sins against the Lord, their rebellion and hardheartedness. Then we read, "*Yet he, being compassionate, atoned for their iniquity and did not destroy them; he restrained his anger often and did not stir up all his wrath*" (Psalm 78:38). Thank God for His compassion!

Jesus, as God's Son, perfectly reflects the Father's compassion. He looked out at a crowd of lost, sinful souls, and "*he had compassion for them, because they were harassed and helpless, like sheep without a shepherd.*" God tells us more about the compassion of Jesus in Hebrews 4:15–16.

> For we do not have a high priest who is unable to sympathize with our weaknesses, but one who in every respect has been tempted as we are, yet without sin. Let us then with confidence draw near to the throne of grace, that we may receive mercy and find grace to help in time of need.

As Christ sees us struggling with sin and falling into temptation, He sympathizes with us. He does not excuse our sin, but He has compassion for us in and through our failures. It is at this point that He proves His love for us. "*God shows his love for us in that while we were still sinners, Christ died for us*" (Romans 5:8). Jesus calls us to imitate Him, therefore God wants to shape in us His heart of compassion for our family members, especially those who are broken and struggling.

Compassion Broke Through

As I have shared, my parents divorced when I was fifteen. I can still remember walking through the halls at school on the day the divorce papers became final. It was surreal. During that next year, my youth pastor, Ken Geis, walked me through the first phase of the forgiveness process. I had to *choose* to forgive my dad. It was not something I wanted to do, nor something I felt that he deserved, but with encouragement I chose to be obedient. "*Forgive as the Lord forgave you*" (Colossians 3:13 NIV).

Then I entered the long road of phase two, forgiveness from the heart. Even though I did not want them, I had no control over my feelings of bitterness and resentment. Those feelings were like a ball and chain around my life that prevented me from having a meaningful ministry to my father, who did not have a relationship with Jesus. Each day I would pray, "Lord, I have chosen to forgive my father. But I can't get rid of these feelings of bitterness and anger. I need you to do that. Change and heal my heart."

This was my daily prayer for six years, and while I didn't always recognize it, the Lord was at work, draining the swamp of my anger. Then came a morning I will never forget. It was my junior year of college, and I was getting ready for a *very* early class, somewhere around eleven in the morning. I was in the bathroom, shaving, and for whatever reason I was thinking about my dad. For the first time in a long time, the emotion that came to the surface was compassion. Normally, if my father was on my mind, compassion was nowhere to be found. But something had changed. God had answered my prayers.

My mind flooded with events from my father's life. He was born during the global influenza pandemic of 1918 in which millions of people died. His mother became sick and died within days of his birth. While we don't know the whole story, his father did not want him. Perhaps he was in grief over the death of his wife or was already feeling overwhelmed with needing to care for his two older sons. My dad lost both his parents. In addition, he was born at seven-and-a-half months. In those times, this type of premature birth was a life-threatening situation. As a result, my father spent the first year of his life in the hospital at the University of Iowa. While I am thankful for the many nurses and doctors who cared for him, that is not the kind of environment a little baby deserves. As a father of seven, I know how precious that first year of life is. A baby is supposed to have the love of a mother, a father, grandparents, and siblings. My dad missed out on all of that.

When he turned one, he was adopted by his uncle and aunt. They were brother and sister, two single people living together for practical reasons. Thank God for his adoption and the care he received, but he never got to see a marriage work. Then, as he was growing up, he received one of the most crippling blows of his entire life. The man who had adopted him, Dean Robert Rienow from the University of Iowa, was a secularist and an educator. He was careful and intentional to impart his world view to my father, and my father sought to pass on some of that instruction to me. Multiple times while I was growing up, my father said to me, "Bobby [he was the only one who called me that], let me tell you the most important lesson the dean taught me: Jesus was just a man."

His mother died. His father did not want him. He had a traumatic infancy. Where do you go to find healing for these deep wounds? Jesus. He is the only one. But your adoptive father tells you, "Jesus was just a man." My father spent his life looking for women to love him. Four wives. Four divorces. Mistresses and girlfriends. He later died with a picture of his mother in his dresser drawer.

All of these painful realities about my father's life came to my mind, and I was filled with *compassion* for him. It was all so sad. Of course, he was responsible for his sins and bad choices. But my dad was a textbook case of the modern proverb, "Hurt people hurt people." The Lord had drained the anger and bitterness out of my heart and replaced it with His compassion. My father was harassed and helpless, like a sheep without a shepherd. The Lord's work in my life enabled me to take steps to seek a better relationship with him and be bolder in my Christian witness.

Sometime after this, I was out to breakfast with him, and I asked him, "Dad, I wonder if you are angry with God for allowing your mom to die when you were born?" Immediately a tear came down his cheek, and predictably he changed the subject to the Boston Red Sox. It was amazing to me. One question about his mother brought him to tears. His wounds were still open because he had never come to the only One who could heal them.

Compassion, Big and Small

We not only need Christ's compassion for our family members in situations of major conflict, but also in day-to-day life. Do you ever have a bad day? Maybe you woke up on the wrong side of the bed or you are feeling a little under the weather.

> We need to ask God to give us His heart of compassion for our family members.

When you are having one of those days, what are you looking for from your family members? Compassion! We want people to show us a little bit of understanding. "I know I am stressed out today, but please don't freak out. Just cut me some slack."

I struggle with putting this into practice with my children. When I am having a bad day, I expect everyone to be understanding and give me a little extra grace. The reality is that *everyone* has bad days. But do I ever allow my children to have them? Do I give them the same respect and understanding I expect others to give me when I am stressed, overwhelmed, or just feeling a little off? I am in for a very frustrating life if I become annoyed and angry every time one of my children or family members does something wrong. We need to ask God to give us His heart of compassion for our family members so that we are not crushed by a spirit of anger, so we can seek peace in response to conflict.

Compassion for the Broken

Matt and Janelle were in shock. Their twenty-five-year-old daughter, Angela, had just informed them that she was a lesbian and was moving in with her partner. Angela also had told her two older siblings, one of whom had reacted in anger, the other in silence. The announcement was the culmination of many warning signs and previous conversations. But despite the years of conflict and dialogue about Angela's identity, attractions, and sexual choices, it now seemed like a line had been crossed. This was real.

Mom and Dad had every normal emotion you would expect from Christian parents. The talk with Angela did not last long, since Matt and Janelle's emotions were too raw for them to provide much of a response. It ended awkwardly but cordially, with the parents asking if they could have some time to think before talking further.

Two days later, Matt asked Angela if there was a good time for them to talk again. He and Janelle knew they had to approach Angela full of grace and full of truth. Matt was usually better at communicating grace, while Janelle was better at the truth. When they met, they told Angela how much they loved her and that they were committed to her—no matter what (full of grace). They also clearly expressed their concern for her, that they did not believe this was God's plan for her, and that these decisions were going to bring her pain and not happiness (full of truth). It was not an easy conversation. Angela appreciated the "full of grace" portion but felt judged by the "full of truth." However, Matt and Janelle noticed that the Lord had done something important in each of their hearts. They were not angry with Angela! Instead, their hearts were filled with *compassion* for her. They were brokenhearted for her as they saw her confusion, her struggles, and the intense spiritual battle she was facing.

They are now walking the long road of talking, praying, crying, and maintaining the best relationship possible with their daughter. Even though Angela is telling them she is happy with the life she has chosen, they see her struggles and pain. Her parents know that the path she is on does not lead to happiness and wholeness. They have made the commitment to parent with a question on the forefront of their minds: "How can we build the kind of relationship with Angela in the months and years ahead that when she crashes—when she hits a wall, when things fall apart—we will be the first people she calls?"

Compassion for the Lost

Sonya was fed up with Ellie. Their relationship as sisters had been rocky since childhood, and now in their thirties things were getting even worse. They did not grow up in a Christian home, but Sonya was born again through a campus ministry in college. Over the years, both sisters had done many things to cause damage to the relationship, including large portions of jealousy, competitiveness, backstabbing, and lying.

After Sonya became a Christian, the Lord helped her take steps to improve the relationship with her sister. She apologized for some of the nasty things she had done. She confessed her jealousy. While Sonya continued to struggle with some mean-spirited behavior toward Ellie, there was improvement. However, Ellie's attitude toward Sonya continued to worsen. At family gatherings, she either avoided Sonya or was outright rude to her. When Sonya posted pictures online, Ellie would leave sarcastic comments. When they did talk, it seemed as if Ellie's top priority was to brag about her accomplishments.

Sonya had had enough. This pattern of behavior from Ellie was unacceptable. She thought, *How can my sister treat me like this? What is her problem? Okay, so we have had our issues, but all sisters have issues. Why can't she just try being nice to me?* That question, "What's her problem?" kept coming into Sonya's mind. Her anger was growing. It was during a prayer time when she sensed the Lord breaking through and answering her question! *What is Ellie's problem? She is dead in her sins. She is not born again. She has not received forgiveness and does not have a relationship with Christ. She is acting spiritually dead because she* is *spiritually dead.*

As the Lord convicted Sonya of this truth, she recognized her judgmental spirit toward her sister and that she had been wrongly expecting someone who was not a believer to act like someone who was. (This is not meant to imply that Christians always act like Christians.) With this vital insight, the Lord filled her heart with more compassion for Ellie. She began to pray in new ways. Instead of praying for God to "make their relationship better," she asked the Lord to "work in Ellie's life and bring her to faith in Christ. Use me as a light for Christ in our relationship." Their relationship continues to be messy. Sonya has needed to establish some boundaries to limit her exposure to some of Ellie's toxic patterns, yet this fresh spirit of compassion has enabled Sonya to have more peace and hope for their future reconciliation.

Let me offer a strong warning here for parents. A few days ago, I spoke with a father on the phone about some serious issues they were facing with their teenage son. The father was fed up with the long list of lies, alcohol use, and disrespect. He yelled at his son, "Maybe the problem here is that you are just not a Christian!" It is possible that the father in this situation was correct. Maybe his son had not responded to the grace of

> A judgmental spirit and compassion
> can't occupy the same space.

God with repentance in faith and was still in his sins. However, an angry pronouncement like this will, in my judgment, only cause severe harm to your child and to your relationship. As I spoke with this father, he had already sensed this and was preparing to go back to his son to ask for his forgiveness. If, as parents, we are concerned that one of our children is not saved, that should never be a cause for anger but for an overwhelming spirit of compassion. Do you see a sinful nature in your children? Remind yourself from whom they inherited it.

Take Action

If we want Christ's heart of compassion for our family members, we need to ask for it. He is the one who changes our hearts. A judgmental spirit and compassion can't occupy the same space. Consider making the following prayer a part of your daily routine for the next few weeks.

Lord, I confess that I struggle with anger and a judgmental spirit toward _____. Remind me that he/she is a person who has been hurt and that some of what they do is a response to what they have experienced. Please give me Christ's heart of compassion. Drive away any harsh or judgmental spirit in me. In the name of Jesus, amen.

Questions for Reflection and Discussion

1. In what ways have you seen the principle "hurt people hurt people" play out in your family?
2. Have you ever experienced a friend or family member showing you compassion, even when you were behaving badly? What impact did that have in your life and on your relationship?
3. Spend some time considering the compassion of God toward His children. Read 2 Chronicles 30:9, Psalm 103:13, and Isaiah 54:10. Talk to the Lord in prayer, thanking Him for His continued compassion toward you, and ask Him to give you that same heart toward your family.

Chapter 9

Healing through Patience

Put on then, as God's chosen ones, holy and beloved, compassionate hearts, kindness, humility, meekness, and patience.

Colossians 3:12

Many times I have had to utter the words, "I am sorry I lost my patience." It is a strange phrase. I had my patience, and I don't know what happened. But I lost it. I don't know where it went. If you find it, let me know! Patience is an essential ingredient in family healing. "All wounds heal over time." Have you heard this before? It sounds nice, but it is not true. If a serious injury is untreated and ignored, time will only make it worse. We can say, however, "God can heal all wounds over time." In this chapter, we will turn our attention to the "over time" aspect of healing relationships. If we want to see healing in our families, we will likely need an extra portion of patience. While learning to be patient with people is helpful, our primary focus here will be our need to grow in patience with God.

God Is Patient with Us

"*God is love*" (1 John 4:8). This is a Scripture we teach to children from their earliest years. Because God is love, one of His essential attributes is patience. "*Love is patient*" (1 Corinthians 13:4). One of the great ways God shows His love to you and me is by being patient with us. Can you imagine what our relationship with God would look like if He were not patient with us?

Do you have anyone in your family who just won't change? He won't grow up. She won't stop doing stupid stuff. He says he is going to stop, but he keeps right on going. Her personality just drives you nuts. How many of us just get fed up, sick of it, and say, "I can't take it anymore"? Maybe we don't say it out loud, but we say it in our hearts. We walk away from a conversation or we hang up the phone, and in our hearts we say, "I am so done with you."

Did you know God never thinks that way about His children? He is the Father who never loses His patience with His kids. Even when God disciplines us, He does so with a spirit of patience. I would have given up on me a long time ago. How many times have I committed the same sin? How many times have I come to God and confessed? I tell Him I don't want to do that again and even vow, "Lord, I promise I will never do that again." Yet how often do I continue to fail?

At some point, we might think God would get fed up with us. I know I would. But when it comes to His children, He never stops caring, loving, and pursuing. He is patient with us, because He loves us.

God Calls Us to Be Patient with Him

Jesus said that the greatest commandment is to "*Love the Lord your God with all your heart*" (Luke 10:27). If love is patient, then part of what it means to love God is that we are to be patient with Him. Consider these Scriptures.

Be still before the Lord and wait patiently for him.

Psalm 37:7

You also, be patient. Establish your hearts, for the coming of the Lord is at hand.

James 5:8

I think every Christian struggles to some degree when it comes to unanswered prayers. We pray for weeks, months, years, and nothing seems to happen. Where is God? What is He doing? Why is He not doing anything? Is He even listening?

When my son Rush was four years old, he said to me, "Daddy, I don't like after."

"What?"

"I don't like after."

"Rush, what do you mean?"

"Dessert is after dinner. Video games are after school. Games are after cleanup. I don't like *after*."

I agree with Rush! I don't like *after*. I like now. But no good parent gives their child everything they ask for *now*. Sometimes a good parent says "no," or sometimes a good parent says "wait." Part of what it means to love God is being patient with Him. This is especially true when it comes to being patient with His work in healing our family relationships. Reconciliation is usually a *slow work* of God.

I enjoy grilling and barbecuing. A few times I have tried smoking a pork shoulder or ribs. I have failed more times than I have succeeded and for one simple reason. I struggle with patience. My philosophy of cooking is "double the heat, half the time." When God brings healing to a relationship, He usually does His work "low and slow" (a common barbecue term). Impatience can ruin a good dinner, as well as a reconciliation process with someone in our family.

What I am going to say here may sound trite or simplistic. It is, in fact, the opposite. In order for us to be patient with God, we have to *trust* Him. I don't mean trusting God in some kind of generic religious sense. I mean literally, genuinely trusting Him. Believing and holding fast to the truth that He loves me.

> He will only allow things into
> my life that He plans to use
> for my ultimate good.

He knows my future. He is never out of control. He will only allow things into my life that He plans to use for my ultimate good. This is the only way to have hope when a family situation seems humanly hopeless.

As believers in Jesus Christ, we have *good reason* to trust God. He sent His Son, who took our sins, died in our place, was raised from the dead, and now lives in our hearts. He is preparing heaven for us. He has promised to return, create a new earth, and give us new bodies, and we will live a perfect, happy life with Him and all His children forever and ever. That is what our God has done and what He is going to do. We start there, and then we turn our attention to the struggles, pain, and sorrow of today.

A Twenty-Year Story of Family Healing

Jacob and Esau had an epic brother-versus-brother conflict. They were twin boys, with Esau being born first. Jacob came out of the womb hanging on to Esau's heel! The conflict between the brothers was fueled by their parents, Isaac and Rebekah. Isaac favored Esau, and Rebekah favored Jacob (Genesis 25:28). The family conflicts intensified when Esau, at the age of forty, chose to marry two Hittite women who "were a source of grief" to Isaac and Rebekah (Genesis 26:34–35 NIV). When it came time for Isaac to bless Esau and transfer the leadership of the family to him, Rebekah helped Jacob deceive his father so that he might receive the blessing rather than his brother. Esau was enraged and "*held a grudge against Jacob because of the blessing his father had given him. He said to himself, 'The days of mourning for my father are near; then I will kill my brother Jacob'*" (Genesis 27:41 NIV). Rebekah helped Jacob escape the wrath of his brother by sending him to live in Haran with his extended family.

Twenty years went by. Both Jacob's and Esau's families grew. Jacob sent a messenger to his brother to see if perhaps his anger had waned. "*The messengers returned to Jacob, saying, 'We came to your brother Esau, and he is coming to meet you, and there are four hundred men with him'*" (Genesis 32:6). Jacob was afraid and rightly so. Was this a welcome party or a war party? Jacob lifted up a humble prayer.

> "O God of my father Abraham and God of my father Isaac, O Lord who said to me, 'Return to your country and to your kindred, that I may do you good,' I am not worthy of the least of all the deeds of steadfast love and all the faithfulness that you have shown to your servant, for with only my staff I crossed this Jordan, and now I have become two camps. Please deliver me from the hand of my brother, from the hand of Esau, for I fear him, that he may come and attack me, the mothers with the children. But you said, 'I will surely do you good, and make your offspring as the sand of the sea, which cannot be numbered for multitude.'"
>
> Genesis 32:9–12

When Jacob's caravan was still far away, he sent three teams of his servants, one after the other, to present gifts to Esau (Genesis 32:13–21). Finally, the time had come for Jacob and Esau to meet face-to-face.

> And Jacob lifted up his eyes and looked, and behold, Esau was coming, and four hundred men with him. So he divided the children among Leah and Rachel and the two female servants. And he put the servants with their children in front, then Leah with her children, and Rachel and Joseph last of all. He himself went on before them, bowing himself to the ground seven times, until he came near to his brother. But Esau ran to meet him and embraced him and fell on his neck and kissed him, and they wept.
>
> Genesis 33:1–4

Esau received the gifts at Jacob's urging and offered to help Jacob's family settle in a safe place (Genesis 33:11–15). It was a fresh start. It was a miracle twenty years in the making.

Don't Judge God from the Middle of the Story

When we are experiencing conflict with a family member, we are in the middle of the story. We don't know what God will do tomorrow as we pray for and seek healing with our families. We can be tempted to judge God based on the middle of the story and focus only on our current painful circumstance.

There was a time in Moses's life when God told him to put his hand into his cloak. Moses did it, and when he took his hand out, it was covered in leprosy. Isn't that terrible? He did what God told him to do and he got leprosy. What kind of a God would do that? If you know the history from Exodus 4, you know that is not the end of the story. God tells Moses to put his hand back into his cloak, and when he removes it, the leprosy is gone.

Joseph had ten older brothers. They were so jealous of him that they sold him into slavery and told their father that he had been eaten by wild animals. Joseph was in prison in Egypt for years. What kind of God would allow that to happen? God obviously did not love or care for Joseph. You are probably saying, "But, Rob, that is not the end of the story!" You would be right. God elevates Joseph to second-in-command in Egypt and uses him to save millions, including his own family, from the famine. He reconciles with his brothers and is reunited with his father. It's awesome—it's amazing. *You can't stop the story when Joseph is in jail!*

One more example. God sends His own Son, Jesus, into the world. He never does anything wrong. Yet He is betrayed, arrested, tortured, and hung on a cross for six hours before He dies. What kind of God would let that happen to His Son? Why didn't He stop it? Hopefully you see the pattern here. When you tell the history of Jesus, you don't end on Friday. You have to get to Sunday morning! Jesus busts out of the grave and is alive today. We even call it *Good* Friday, in light of Sunday's resurrection.[1]

This principle applies as we face our family struggles. In this moment we are suffering and feeling lonely, rejected, and hopeless. But this is just the middle of the story. Let's not judge God in the middle, but instead trust Him, patiently and completely, to accomplish His good purposes in His good timing.

Speed It Up, God!

Another area where I struggle is being patient with God in light of His tardiness in sanctifying those around me. I believe in the work of the Holy Spirit to make us more like Christ, but I just think He could be working a little faster on a few key people in my life.

Amy and I have seven children, so I live with eight other people. Granted, that number is dropping as more of our children are launching into the college years and beyond. But as I am writing these words, all the kids are home on summer break. By the grace of God, each one of our children has put their faith in Christ, but we all continue to struggle with sin. I wake up each day facing the daunting prospect of making it through the day with eight sinful people living under my roof. You can imagine how difficult my life must be! Technically, there are nine sinners in the family, with myself as sinner in chief, but I prefer to focus on their problems. Hopefully the humor is coming through here.

As a parent, it is easy to become frustrated with the lack of progress we see in our kids' growth. *When will he learn to keep his room clean? When will she stop being so defensive? When will he pay attention to the speed limit? When will she stop picking on her little sister?* It is easy for me to get exasperated with the slow character growth in my kids or my wife while I simultaneously offer myself a pass for areas of my life that are not progressing. As long as I am "trying" or "doing my best" to change a bad habit, I expect grace, tolerance, and even affirmation from my wife and kids.

If we want our believing family members to be gracious to us in regard to the slow growth God is bringing about in our lives, we must strive to be patient with God's slow work in their hearts as well. I have to remind myself, *This person is not my project! They are God's project. I am not sanctifying them by my "holy spirit," God is sanctifying them by His Holy Spirit.*

God Works behind the Scenes

I hope we can all agree that God is working in our families in a myriad of ways that we do not see. He may be doing a healing work right now in one of your family relationships, and yet it may not be revealed for months or years to come. A few years ago, when Rush, our youngest son, was two, we did the big Disney World trip. We had done the full day, all the way through the evening fireworks, and it was now time to wait in line for the monorail, and then wait in another line for the bus, until finally we returned to our condo. Rush fell asleep during this one-hour transportation saga. The place where we were staying didn't have a ton of room, so the plan was for Rush to sleep in the same queen bed with Amy and me. The problem was that he was covered in "theme park juices." Sweat. Drool. Ice cream. Candy. There was no way I was going to sleep with *that*. So I laid him, still sound asleep, down on the bed. I took off his clothes and carried him into the shower with me. I cleaned him head to toe, and he never woke up. After drying him off, I laid him back on the bed and put his pajamas on him. He did not wake up until morning.

Rush had no clue he was filthy. He was sound asleep through the whole cleaning process. He just woke up and it was done. Our heavenly Father often works the same way, working in secret, quietly, to create healing and cleansing in our families. This is why it's so important to trust Him and be patient with Him.

I remember talking with a mom named Cindy at one of our Never Too Late seminars. She told me about her adult daughter, who lived in Arizona. Her daughter had moved away from the family, declared herself an atheist, and cut off all contact with her mother. At the conference, we talked about the power of writing letters of blessing to our children. The letter has two simple paragraphs, one in which you tell your child how much you love God, and the second in which you tell your child how much you love them.[2] Writing letters of blessing and affirmation to our children can make a powerful impact in their lives. It is *godly* parenting in that our heavenly

Father chose to put His love for us in writing in the pages of the Bible.

Cindy told me there was no point in her writing the letter. Her daughter would just throw it away. She didn't answer her calls, texts, or emails, so why would she open a letter? I said, "You may be right. Writing the letter may be a waste of an hour, but you can waste an hour watching Netflix too." With that prompting, she decided to send the letter. And just as Cindy expected, there was no response. Two years later, God worked a miracle in her daughter's heart, restoring her relationships with God and her family. Her daughter shared with Cindy the story of her transformation. "Mom, do you know when all this started? When I got your letter. At the time, I didn't want you to know that I received the letter or that I read it . . . or that I cared. But that letter was the first step toward God changing my heart." During those years of separation, and the two years following the sending of the letter, Cindy had to seek healing through patience.

My Worst Fruit

God puts *patience* first in the list of His definition of love. Love is patient. He gives it to us again in Galatians 5:22–23: "*But the fruit of the Spirit is love, joy, peace, patience, kindness, good-ness, faithfulness, gentleness, self-control; against such things there is no law.*" I served for many years as a youth pastor. One of my patterns was that, at the end of each year of ministry, I would ask my fifty volunteers to evaluate me, my performance, and my leadership. One of the things I asked them to do was to tell me to what degree they saw these nine fruits of the Spirit in my life. I did this for about five years, and every time the same virtue came out on the bottom. You guessed it. Patience was always the "least seen" character trait in my life. So I stopped doing the survey! If I already know what you are going to tell me, that I am impatient, why waste time doing a survey just to be told I'm impatient? Time to hurry up and move to the next thing.

Being Patient versus Looking Patient

Because this is my worst fruit, God gives extra Holy Spirit attention to me in this area. Here is something the Lord has convicted me of: Just because I can *hide* my impatience does not mean I am being loving and patient. I was recently in the checkout line at Panera, along with a couple of my younger kids. Our server was pleasant, friendly, and moving more slowly than I would have preferred.

"Can I help you?"

"Yeah, I would like two muffins, two croissants, and a large coffee."

"So . . . that will be . . . two . . . muf . . . fins . . . two . . . croi . . . ssants . . . and one . . . large . . . cof . . . fee. Can I read your order back to you?"

"No, thank you. I'm quite confident you got it. Thank you very much."

I proceeded to pay and pick up the order, and as I was walking out the door with my kids in tow, I said, "That was unbelievable! Someone needs to pick up the pace around here." Let's pretend that I fooled the kind person behind the register with my politeness. But I didn't fool my kids, and I certainly didn't fool God. God tells us that love *is* patient, not that love *looks* patient. It is an internal command for our hearts, not merely an external command for our words and behavior. Here I need to regularly say, "Lord, forgive me."

We can focus our action prayers in this direction. Let's not pray, "God help me to act more patiently with my husband," or

"Help me to show more patience toward my sister," but rather, "Lord, make my heart more patient. Align my heart with yours.

> Lord, give me the same loving
> patience for my family members
> that you show toward me.

Give me the same loving patience for my family members that you show toward me."

Extra Patience Required

There is a common family situation that requires a "special ministry" of patience. Tom and Michelle have three married children and five grandchildren (and counting). Michelle's parents lived about an hour away, and for the past few years they had been in declining health. Unexpectedly, her father passed away after a bout with pneumonia and related complications. Up until that time, her mom's mental health was not great but manageable, but then with the death of her husband she rapidly declined.

Tom and Michelle began traveling back and forth multiple times each week to provide support and practical help to her mom, who was still in her home. It was clear, however, that new living arrangements were needed for her. Those conversations were not easy. To make matters worse, when Michelle's mom was not having a good day, she was increasingly angry and belligerent. This was not typical behavior for her, and it was obvious that a lot of this new mean streak was being driven by her mental illness.

It has now been almost five years since Michelle's dad went home to be with the Lord. Mom now lives in a care facility, and it is increasingly difficult to connect with her. As Tom and Michelle watched her regress, almost to a childlike state, the Lord gave them a critical insight. Caring for Mom was a ministry given to them by God in this season of their lives, and it was, to a great degree, a ministry of *patience*. They were "making some return" (see 1 Timothy 5:4) to Michelle's mom for her years of raising Michelle when she was a child. Raising a child is a ministry of patience, and so is caring for an aging parent—especially in a season of physical or mental decline.

Patience with Persistence

The call to patience is not a call to passivity. As a father, I want to have loving, heart-connected relationships with my children. But those kinds of relationships don't just happen. I have been encouraged by the following words from Dennis Rainey:

> A teenage boy can come out on the other side of adolescence as a man . . . if this man-in-the-making is trained by the right kind of man. . . . A man who recognizes the dangers in our culture and does his duty . . . despite the intense pressures he faces. The greatest pressures you will face as a father are your son's tendency to "push back" or resist your involvement and your temptation to "pull out" or disengage from his life.
>
> Pressure no. 1: The Push Back. It's not easy to be involved in your son's life during his adolescent years. As he steps out of boyhood, he doesn't know how to become a man, and he has little experience of the lethal temptations he will confront. But his desire for independence will lead him to begin pushing you out of his life. . . . He'll argue with you and stiff-arm you. . . . He will think he knows more than you.
>
> Pressure no. 2: The Pull Out. What makes the teenage years exponentially perilous is that at the same time your son and his peers are pushing back, you'll see many fathers beginning to

pull out of their sons' lives. The exhaustion that comes at the end of a pressure-packed workday can result in passivity. . . . The antidote to the Push Back and the Pull Out is to continue pressing in. . . . As a man you must courageously step up and stay involved, wisely moving deeper into your son's life even as you are pressured to step out of it.[3]

Patience in Maintaining Boundaries

Earlier, you heard the story of Kelly and Marcus and Kelly's process of setting up healthy boundaries to help her adult son. If you need to implement any kind of boundary with a family member, patience will be an essential ingredient. First, ask the Lord to help you be patient with yourself. Often we come to a place of needing to set boundaries because we have not set them properly in the past. We are learning new ways of relating to our family. This is not an easy process. We easily slip into old patterns of enabling or allowing ourselves to be taken advantage of. Be patient with yourself. Second, ask the Lord to help you be patient with the boundaries process. Don't withdraw your boundaries at the first sign of trouble, anger, or rejection. When Kelly first implemented the boundaries with Marcus, the conversation did not go well. Now at the sixth-month mark, while the situation has not miraculously transformed, there have been small steps toward peace. It is vital that Kelly continue to stay the course and be patient with the boundaries process.

Seeking healing through patience does *not* mean being patient with an abuser. If you or your family members are in a dangerous situation, it is not time for patience. Get Christian counsel immediately and do what is necessary to get yourself and others into a safe environment. Then, from an emotional (and physical if necessary) place of safety, ask God to fill your heart with patience as you seek healing and reconciliation.

Questions for Reflection and Discussion

1. How would your life be different if God did not show His love for you through patience?

2. Which one of your family members do you have the least patience with? Why do you think that is? Commit yourself to praying for God to give you more patience for this person.

3. Can you think of examples in your life where God answered prayer quickly? On the other side, are there some prayers in your life right now that God does not seem to be answering? For those areas where God is acting slowly, ask Him to give you patience with Him and greater trust in His plan for the future of your family.

Chapter 10

Healing through Mediators

> Where there is no guidance, a people falls, but in an abundance of counselors there is safety.
>
> Proverbs 11:14

"We don't air our dirty laundry." My dad was fond of this phrase. "We don't talk about our family problems with other people. Private matters should stay private." While there is value in appropriate confidentiality, this mind-set often leads families to struggle in solitude when they could (and should) reach out for help and support. Through our years of counseling couples, Amy and I have lost track of the number of times we have said, "If only they had reached out for help sooner! The first call they made was *after* they had decided to divorce." Seeking godly counsel from your pastor, a Christian counselor, or a trusted friend is not a sign of weakness, but rather a sign of maturity and strength.

None of us is eager to invite others into our struggles and messed-up families. We come by this honestly. In response to his sin, our first father, Adam, hid from God and blamed both Eve and God for his own disobedience. We all have been hiding and blaming ever since. Asking for help with our family problems brings up a spirit of shame. *No one else in our church seems to have these problems. I just couldn't handle it if people were to find out what's really going on in this family. We don't need help from anyone.*

I was preaching in our home church, and I mentioned, as a part of my sermon, that Amy and I had recently gone to see a marriage counselor to talk about some communication problems we were having. It was a side comment, and I did not elaborate on the details. After church, I had two similar conversations. These congregation members were a bit taken aback that their pastor and his wife went to see a counselor *and* that this had been mentioned from the pulpit. This led to a great conversation.

"It was unusual to hear a pastor say that he and his wife went to marriage counseling. I'm not saying it was bad—I am just not sure I have heard anything like that before."

I responded, "Marriage is awesome, but it is also hard, and Amy and I have our struggles like every other couple. Sometimes we just get stuck in a conflict or communication pattern, and we can't seem to find a way out. It would be nice if we could make it through our problems without help, but that is just not reality for us. We get in spots where 'we can't see the forest for the trees.' Sadly, I am not very objective about our issues and the things I'm doing to make things worse. Sometimes it takes a godly, outside person to show me a better way to think or things I need to do differently."

No One Ever Asked

Bob and Lenore had been attending our church for a few months, and I was looking forward to getting to know their family.

They had come from a very small fellowship, fewer than fifty people, where they had been worshiping for the past ten years. Their previous church had been committed to systematic Bible study, which was the primary focus of their Sunday and other gatherings.

We met for coffee, and I enjoyed learning about their faith journey, their previous church family, and the ups and downs of their family life. After about forty-five minutes of conversation, I asked, "How are things going in your marriage?" Awkward pause. Lenore quietly said, "To be honest, we are having some struggles. And . . . no one has ever asked."

I was stunned, but not by the fact that they were struggling in their marriage. One hundred percent of married couples have problems. That is what happens when two sinners get together. *But no one had ever asked?* They had spent more than

> The gospel message centers
> on what God has done to
> reconcile sinners to himself.

ten years in a small Christian church. They had been meeting with the same people week after week, year after year, talking about God's Word and spiritual things, yet no one had asked them, "How is your marriage going?"

Sadly, this may be the norm rather than the exception. Do you have a few trusted friends who care for you enough to ask you how things are going at home? Do you trust them enough to answer honestly? Is there a pastor from your church who is seeking to personally encourage you in your family life? As my wife has observed these patterns in the church and in our community, she has said to me, "So many people are living lonely lives full of people."

God Sent a Mediator

The gospel message centers on what God has done to reconcile sinners to himself. He is the Father seeking to heal the broken relationship with His children, even though His children were the ones who broke (and continue to break) the relationship. What did our heavenly Father do to reconcile us to himself? He sent His Son as a mediator.

> For there is one God, and there is one mediator between God and men, the man Christ Jesus, who gave himself as a ransom for all, which is the testimony given at the proper time.
>
> 1 Timothy 2:5–6

> He [Jesus] entered once for all into the holy places, not by means of the blood of goats and calves but by means of his own blood, thus securing an eternal redemption. . . . Therefore he is the mediator of a new covenant, so that those who are called may receive the promised eternal inheritance, since a death has occurred that redeems them from the transgressions committed under the first covenant.
>
> Hebrews 9:12, 15

One of the most powerful cries for a mediator comes from Job. He had lost his children, his wealth, and his health. Why had God allowed this to happen? He knew that God was the all-powerful Creator and that he had no right to question Him. Consider his words from Job 9:32–33: "*For he [God] is not a man, as I am, that I might answer him, that we should come to trial together. There is no arbiter between us, who might lay his hand on us both.*" Job knows that the only way he could ever draw close to God would be through an *arbiter*, or mediator. He needed someone who could put one hand on the "shoulder" of God and his other hand on the shoulder of man. But who could do this? Who could ever be fully divine and fully human at the same time? Enter Jesus! From before the creation of the world, God had a plan to send His Son to mediate and to reconcile and ransom a sinful people to himself.

God made one, and only one, way for sinful men and women to be reconciled to Him, and that is through the *mediation* of His Son. You may have heard the statement "We are not saved by works." That sentence is incomplete. It is true that we are not saved by *our* works, but we are most certainly saved by the *work* of Jesus—His coming, His sinless life, His death, and His resurrection. Jesus taught this when He said, "*I am the way, and the truth, and the life. No one comes to the Father except through me*" (John 14:6).

When *our* family relationships are broken, we can follow this gospel example and seek counsel and the ministry of mediators.

Jesus Taught Us to Seek Help from Mediators

Seeking counsel and mediation for our family conflict is not only wise, but in some cases Jesus commands it. In Matthew 18, Jesus gives careful instructions for how we should respond when someone sins against us. This may be a familiar passage to you. Unfortunately, it is often referred to as "the church discipline passage." While church discipline is addressed here, it is only a subset of Jesus' focus. His primary focus is to provide His people with a practical step-by-step plan to seek reconciliation when relationships are broken.

In verse 15, Jesus begins, "*If your brother sins against you, go and tell him his fault, between you and him alone. If he listens to you, you have gained your brother.*" Because this passage has been used to focus on church relationships, we often miss something obvious. When Jesus says "brother," that is not just

137

some New Testament spiritual term meaning "your brother in Christ at church." Your "brother" may refer to your biological brother. That's right. The guy you grew up with. If Jesus' instructions apply to our relationships at church, they certainly apply to our relationships at home.[1]

Step 1—Have a Direct Conversation

What should you do if your brother offends you? Jesus says to go to him, personally and privately, and directly tell your brother what he did that hurt you. Before we consider engaging an outside mediator, Jesus instructs us to seek reconciliation privately. Many times in our counseling ministry we have heard people unpack a difficult and conflictual situation with a family member. We typically ask, "When was the last time you directly talked with your brother about this problem and your hurt feelings?" Far too often the answer comes back, "Well, I have not really talked with him directly." Jesus says that a private conversation is the place to start.

I realize that Jesus didn't have to navigate the world of texting and email, but I would strongly suggest that any conversation along these lines be in person, or at the very least over the

> Many family relationships are broken and struggling because of a lack of loving, direct conversations.

phone. If you attempt to have an important, personal, emotional conversation via text or email, it will go badly 99.99 percent of the time. If you want to add more fuel to the fire in a tense situation, send a text. If you want to take a step toward healing, make a call or find a time to talk face-to-face.

Many family relationships are broken and struggling because of a lack of loving, direct conversations. "Hey, the other day when you made that joke in front of my friends, it hurt my feelings. I was looking for a good time to talk with you about it. Sorry it took me a couple of days. But I want things to be right between us, so I needed to tell you." In a healthy family, conversations like this are normal. In unhealthy families, they may not even be *allowed*.

Is Jesus' Goal Your Goal?

According to Jesus, what is the goal of this personal, direct conversation? *Gaining your brother.* In other words, the purpose is healing and reconciliation. The goal is a win for the relationship, not winning the argument. Before we have a step-one conversation with our spouse, parent, or child, we need to do a "heart check." *Do I want to have this conversation to seek healing or to be right? Am I bringing this up for the sake of peace or to make war? Am I coming with a spirit of humility or superiority? Do I want to put this conflict behind us or rub my brother's nose in it?*

If your goal is to *gain your brother*, consider sharing your concern with "the sandwich approach." This is a communication plan that clearly emphasizes your commitment to your family member and to your relationship. The "sandwich" part is *love, truth, love.* I am thankful that Amy often employs this approach when talking with me about conflicts in our relationship. She might say:

> Rob, thanks for being willing to talk with me. I love you, and I am committed to our marriage. [Love.] I need to be honest with you. When you forget to lock the cars at night, after telling me you will do it, it makes me feel unsafe because people can

use the garage door openers in the cars to get into the house. It is hard to trust you when you say you will do something and then don't do it. [Truth.] I want to work through this together, and I love you. [Love.]

I am like any other sinful person. I don't like to be confronted. I don't like it when others shine a light on my mistakes. But when Amy affirms her love and commitment to me, it encourages me to give a softer, more humble response. You might consider writing down your love-truth-love sandwich before your conversation with a family member. It doesn't need to be long. In fact, there is power in being clear and concise about your love, commitment, *and* concern.

Let me remind you of a principle from the chapter on repentance. As we look at Jesus' words here in Matthew 18, there is a focus on how to respond when someone has sinned against us. However, if our conflict is a two-way street, it would be wise for your first direct, private conversation to be focused on taking responsibility for what you have done to contribute to the breakdown in the relationship. It may be that your repentance opens the door for your family member to respond with their own confession of what they did to hurt you.

Step 2—Ask Mediators to Help

What if your family member responds badly to your direct conversation? Jesus gives us the next step: *"But if he does not listen, take one or two others along with you, that every charge may be established by the evidence of two or three witnesses"* (Matthew 18:16).

The wheels frequently fall off here at this second step. First, it requires great love even to be obedient to Jesus' instruction. "Look, I talked with my sister. It didn't go well. In fact, I think it made things worse. She is angrier, and I am even more frustrated!" If Jesus' step one failed, why would we take the risk of going to step two?

The process can also fall apart at this step, because true motives may be revealed. If we choose to reach out for mediation, our instinct is to find people who will be sympathetic to our side. If we are going to bring other people into our fight, we want them to help us win. Remember, it's a rare family conflict that is 100 percent the fault of one person and 0 percent the fault of the other. The "win" when we reach out to mediators is that we take a step toward healing, humility, and reconciliation, not vindication of our perspective or self-righteousness. Therefore, we should think carefully about which two or three people to reach out to for help. Here are some questions that may help you make a wise invitation:

- Who has a relationship with both of us?
- Who could we trust to give honest feedback and counsel to us without fear of hurting our feelings?
- Do we respect their faith and character such that we would be willing to receive their counsel?
- Do we trust them enough to be honest in our conversation?

There may also be value in asking your family member to play point in choosing the two or three mediators. "I know we tried to work things out when we met last week. I am sorry that didn't go well. I am still committed to reconciling with you and putting this behind us. The next step is for us to get some outside help." (If your family member is a Christian, you could make reference to Matthew 18.) "Would you be willing to choose two or three people we could meet with and who could listen to our situation and help us work things out?"

You might consider asking family (or extended family) members to serve as mediators. It may be that family members have the best insight, and the most love, to offer you. If you choose to ask for help from family members, it is especially important that you do not seek to manipulate the conversation or try to build a coalition for your cause. Otherwise your attempt at reconciliation could do more harm than good.

Triangulation Is Not Mediation

Triangulation is a term used in the counseling world to describe an unhealthy pattern of bringing third parties into personal conflicts. Put simply, when we have a conflict with a family member, the healthiest approach is to address the problem directly with that person. This destructive pattern emerged in the Schneider family. Chris and Julie had two children, one son and one daughter, both of whom were married with children of their own.

Unfortunately, a pattern of triangulating developed when their children were in high school. At the time, Julie began to struggle with misusing alcohol. At first, the drinking occurred at night, but then the bottles started coming out in the daytime hours as well. When she was under the influence, her personality changed and not for the better. Family gatherings became increasingly awkward and unpredictable.

Chris began to express his concerns about his wife's drinking to his accountability partner at church. At times those conversations led to productive prayer, and at other times it felt more like a venting session. Julie's son and daughter talked frequently about the problem with their dad. They shared their frustration, anger, and concern. As the daughter learned more about alcoholism, she posted links and articles on her social-media page. Secretly she hoped that her mom would read her posts, and maybe they would help her.

Over the course of a year, there were many conversations, texts, emails, and prayer requests, yet none of them directly involved Julie. Soon her drinking was a well-publicized "family secret." Sadly, the alcohol issues worsened to the point where an intervention was required. At long last, Chris and the kids asked a Christian counselor to help them, as a group, express their love for Julie and their unified desire for her to get help for her addiction. Unfortunately, the many months of triangulation, and lack of direct loving conversations with Julie, enabled the situation to significantly worsen. Thankfully it's not too late, and the Schneider family is now in an active process of seeking healing and reconciliation.

Step 3—Ask Church Leaders to Help

What do we do if we have tried to have a personal conversation and have also met with mediators, but there is still no progress toward healing? Jesus gives us a third step: "*Take one or two others along with you, that every charge may be established by the evidence of two or three witnesses. If he refuses to listen to them, tell it to the church. And if he refuses to listen even to the church, let him be to you as a Gentile and a tax collector*" (Matthew 18:16–17).

If our family member is a follower of Jesus, and he or she has not responded to a one-on-one effort to seek reconciliation and has rejected the help of mediators, Jesus instructs us to ask our church leaders for help. The reason for this step is that our pastors have spiritual authority in our lives beyond that of the mediators who may have participated in step two. The Lord instructs us in Hebrews 13:17, "*Obey your leaders [in the church] and submit to them, for they are keeping watch over your souls, as those who will have to give account.*"

As noted above, this cannot be done in a spirit of, "Pastor, I need you to straighten out my son. When can we meet?" Rather, "Pastor, my son and I are struggling in our relationship. I am sure we have both contributed to the problems, and we need your help to take some steps toward forgiveness and healing." You can say this even if you think the problems are 99 percent your son's fault. Your 1 percent still matters.

Dave and Crystal were in an unhealthy pattern with Crystal's parents. All four of them were believers and attended the same church together. If Crystal did something to upset her mother, her father, Larry, would become angry and berate her, usually on the phone but sometimes in person. A few attempts were made to resolve the conflict, yet it was going nowhere. It was suggested, and everyone agreed, that they needed outside help, so as a group they made an appointment to meet with their pastor at his office. The pastor did not have a magic wand to fix everything, but the family could communicate more clearly and calmly with one another because the pastor was there to mediate. The meeting did not end with an apology-filled, tearful reconciliation. Still, it was a positive step forward. God blessed their choice to humble themselves and ask for help from the church.

I Don't Know Who to Call

I met Jeremy at one of our Visionary Marriage weekend conferences. His wife, Anne, was there as well, although she did not seem to be particularly engaged. During one of the breaks, Jeremy shared with me the variety of struggles they were facing in their relationship. As I listened, I saw many reasons for hope for their marriage, but there was also an urgent need for additional help. I suggested that, after the conference, he contact one of the pastors at the church to schedule an appointment. He responded, "I don't know who to call." It was an odd response, as he and Anne had been a part of the church for a few years, and there were a couple of pastors on staff who focused on care and counseling. I recommended these two pastors to Jeremy, giving him their names. He then expressed a deeper issue. "I know who those guys are, but I don't have a lot of confidence that they can help me."

Sadly, I have heard this sentiment shared dozens of times over my years in ministry. Sometimes this is just a smokescreen put up by someone who fears the shame of "airing their dirty laundry" to the pastor. It is easy to fall into the deception that your church is filled with perfect people and you are the only messed-up family. But in other situations, there is a true lack of trust and confidence in the maturity and ability of the pastor or pastoral team. Please accept my bluntness here. This is a serious spiritual situation. One of two things may be happening. One possibility is that you are in a state of spiritual arrogance to such a degree that you are unable or unwilling to submit yourself to the shepherds God has placed in your life. The other is that you are in a church headed by immature, unwise, and untrained pastors, in which case you may need to take serious and deliberate steps to find a new church home where you will receive biblical and effective shepherding.

I don't mean to oversimplify matters that can be very complicated, but if we lack confidence in our pastors to the degree that we will not obey Jesus' instruction to reach out to them for help, we should consider this an urgent situation that requires our attention and action.

Wisdom Points on Christian Counseling

Amy and I have been around the Christian counseling world for almost thirty years. Amy has worked as an LCPC (licensed

145

clinical professional counselor) with a focus on marriage and family therapy. Through my experience as a pastor, and our ministry together through Visionary Family Ministries, we have seen the good, the bad, and the ugly in the world of counseling. As you walk through Jesus' instructions from Matthew 18, here are some principles that may help you as you consider engaging a Christian counselor to help your family.

Get counseling as a family unit

"We need to get you into counseling or something. You need help!" In many broken families, one person is identified as the one who needs to be "fixed." While it may be true that one individual's issues are driving a lot of the dysfunction, it is likely that the entire family system—all the relationships together—need to be examined. Consider how different these approaches are. Option one: "I am done with our problems. You need to get some help. I really think you need counseling. Here is a good person for you to call." Option two: "I am exhausted dealing with our conflict and problems. It seems as though we keep going around and around on the same stuff. I think we need help. I know I need help. If I were to call this counselor, would you be willing to go with me?" I think I am on safe ground in my prediction that option two will be more fruitful.

Don't hesitate to go alone

You have heard the phrase "It takes two." When it comes to healing a family relationship, that statement is true in the long term. But in the short term, it only takes one—one person who is seeking reconciliation. If your husband is unwilling to go to Christian counseling with you, then you can go by yourself. You can prioritize *your need* to get help, support, strength, and biblical guidance. Tell your husband, "I would really like for us to get counseling together, but I know that you don't want to go. I have decided to go on my own because I think I need help, I want to become a better wife, and I want to learn things that I can do to build a healthier family."

Go one time

There are all sorts of reasons why you may be hesitant to seek Christian counseling. I have given this encouragement to many people over the years: "Just go once. Give it a try. After the first meeting, you can make a decision about whether to continue with that counselor or if you think you need to try someone else." I am not implying that one session will fix everything (or even anything), but rather that finding a Christian counseling relationship that can help you in the long term starts with a first meeting. If you don't come out of that first meeting with a sense of confidence and personal connection, try someone else.

Create a team

As a pastor, I have walked with many families through deep and complicated conflicts. In these multifaceted situations, I would try to reach out to form a support team, including trusted Christian counselors and caring mentors. A pitfall with these larger, complex situations is that the pastors, counselors, and mentors were not all on the same page. Perhaps the wife was seeing one counselor while the husband was seeing another. With this arrangement, each counselor was hearing only one side of the story. Over time, their individual counselors began to take the side of their client, sometimes at the expense of the marriage.

If you are facing an emergency family situation (such as adultery, abandonment, abuse, or addiction) and you are engaging with multiple Christian counselors, I strongly advise all parties to sign release forms so that the pastors and counselors can freely communicate with one another. When I was doing pastoral counseling, this was something I required of families who were facing serious issues. If I, as the pastor, was going to partner with a Christian counselor to support the family, it was essential that the counselor was legally permitted to share with me his or her perspective on the situation. Creating a formal care team, with the expectation of collaboration, protects the pastors and counselors, but it also gives the family the best chance to reconcile.

Make sure "Christian" means Christian

I don't like including this warning note, but unfortunately it is necessary. Some counselors who advertise themselves as Christians do not base their counseling on the Bible. Or perhaps they put their psychology first and Scripture second. If you are a Christian seeking Christian counseling, it is appropriate to want that counselor, and their guidance, to be distinctively and overtly Christian. It should be normal to have prayer be a part of your time together. The Bible should be referenced, at the very least, if not directly brought to bear on the conversation. Tragically, I have seen people come out of pseudo Christian counseling in worse shape than when they went in. If you are searching for a Christian counselor, begin by getting a recommendation from your pastor or a trusted Christian friend. After your first session, make a prayerful assessment about whether to continue or look for a better fit.

Questions for Reflection and Discussion

1. When you were growing up, how did your family deal with your "dirty laundry"? Was it appropriate to share your struggles and ask for help?

2. The first step in Jesus' teaching in Matthew 18 is to go privately and directly to the person who has sinned against you. While this seems simple, many of us struggle with doing it. What keeps you from being direct with your family members about your conflicts?

3. Consider a family conflict you may be in right now. What is the next step according to Jesus? Once you identify that step, make a plan for how and when you will take it. Consider reaching out to a friend or prayer partner to ask for their support.

Chapter 11

Healing through Mercy

But God, being rich in mercy, because of the great love with which he loved us, even when we were dead in our trespasses, made us alive together with Christ—by grace you have been saved.

Ephesians 2:4–5

The big day was here. It was time for the family garage sale. There are two kinds of garage sales. One is where you're trying to make money, and the other is where you're trying to get rid of as much stuff as possible. This was the latter. The driveway was packed. Everything in the front of the driveway was one dollar apiece, and everything at the back was five dollars apiece—priced to sell! Around lunchtime I had to run an errand, so I put my two daughters in charge, who at the time were ages twelve and nine. Don't worry—my older son, JD, was there to "supervise" as needed. Just as I was getting ready to leave, JD's friend Jay rode his bike into the driveway and parked it, then walked into the house. I saw that Jay's bike was parked right in the middle of the garage-sale stuff, so I quickly asked him to move his bike well out of the way so it would not get sold. After seeing the bike moved, I jumped in the car and headed out to do my errand.

While I was at the store, my cellphone rang. JD was on the line with a panicked voice. "Dad, the girls sold Jay's bike!" Unbelievable. I rushed home. "Jay," I said, "I am so sorry about this. I thought we had moved your bike out of the way, but I should have made sure the girls knew. I can't believe they sold your bike."

"Well, it's not my bike!"

"What do you mean it's not your bike?"

"It's my mom's bike."

Not only was it Jay's mom's bike, but it was also a *new* Trek mountain bike, which had just been sold for five dollars. Someone just got the greatest garage-sale deal in history! So now it was time for me to call Jay's dad.

"Hey, DR . . ."

"Hi, Rob. What's up?"

I went on to tell him the sad tale of his wife's bike getting sold by accident and offered to do whatever was needed to make things right. There was an awkward pause . . . and then DR broke out laughing! (I didn't think it was all that funny.) He could have demanded that I pay him the full price for the bike.

> **Mercy** is choosing not to carry out a
> punishment that is rightly deserved.

That would have been rightly deserved. Instead, he replied, "Don't worry about it. You don't need to pay us for the bike. Here is all I ask. I reserve the right to tell this story to anyone I want to!"

I gratefully accepted his terms, and both Amy and I were incredibly thankful for their *mercy*.

We pray that such mercy will be a defining characteristic of our family and be carried into the future generations. The mercy of God is at the heart of the gospel message, which is *"foolishness to those who are perishing"* (1 Corinthians 1:18 NIV). What is mercy? It is choosing not to carry out a punishment that is rightly deserved.

The Mercy of God

"Lord, have mercy on me, a sinner." Have you ever spoken these words to God? When we come face-to-face with our sinfulness, we become fully aware of our guilt before the Lord. We know that *"all have sinned and fall short of the glory of God"* (Romans 3:23), and that *"the wages of sin is death"* (Romans 6:23). Our only hope is the mercy of God! So we throw ourselves upon His mercy and ask that He would forgive us and not give us the punishment our sins deserve. Here is the gospel message promised in the prophecy of Isaiah 53:5: *"But he was pierced for our transgressions; he was crushed for our iniquities; upon him was the chastisement that brought us peace, and with his wounds we are healed."* The punishment that we deserved was put on Jesus! But we will not and cannot receive the mercy of God without repentance. *"Let the wicked* forsake *his way, and the unrighteous man his thoughts: and let him* return *unto the Lord, and he will have mercy upon him; and to our God, for he will abundantly pardon"* (Isaiah 55:7 KJV, emphasis added).

God's Call for Us to Be Merciful

I hope you have seen an important pattern throughout this book. We can look to the character and behavior of God to find everything we need as we seek healing in our family relationships. We find that pattern again here. God pursues reconciliation with us through mercy, and He calls us to do the same with others. This was a significant and repeated theme in Jesus' teachings. *"Be merciful, even as your Father is merciful"* (Luke 6:36). *"Blessed are the merciful, for they shall receive mercy*" (Matthew 5:7). Jesus repeatedly confronted the Pharisees about their lack of mercy:

> And as Jesus reclined at table in the house, behold, many tax collectors and sinners came and were reclining with Jesus and his disciples. And when the Pharisees saw this, they said to his disciples, "Why does your teacher eat with tax collectors and sinners?" But when he heard it, he said, "Those who are well have no need of a physician, but those who are sick. Go and learn what this means: 'I desire mercy, and not sacrifice.' For I came not to call the righteous, but sinners."
>
> Matthew 9:10–13

Jesus later shared a parable about forgiveness and mercy with His disciples. In this teaching, He gives a serious warning to those who have received mercy but who remain unmerciful. Here are two points of historical context. The first servant owed the king "ten thousand talents," and the second servant owed the first "a hundred denarii." A denarii was worth roughly one day's wages.[1] A talent was the equivalent of 6,000 denarii![2] Therefore, the first servant owed the king 600,000 times more than the second servant owed him. Here is Jesus' parable and His stern warning:

> "Therefore the kingdom of heaven may be compared to a king who wished to settle accounts with his servants. When he began to settle, one was brought to him who owed him ten thousand talents. And since he could not pay, his master ordered him to be sold, with his wife and children and all that he had, and payment to be made. So the servant fell on his knees, imploring him, 'Have patience with me, and I will pay you everything.' And out of pity for him, the master of that servant released him and forgave him the debt. But when that same servant went out, he found one of his fellow servants who owed him a hundred denarii, and seizing him, he began to choke him, saying, 'Pay

what you owe.' So his fellow servant fell down and pleaded with him, 'Have patience with me, and I will pay you.' He refused and went and put him in prison until he should pay the debt. When his fellow servants saw what had taken place, they were greatly distressed, and they went and reported to their master all that had taken place. Then his master summoned him and said to him, 'You wicked servant! I forgave you all that debt because you pleaded with me. And should not you have had mercy on your fellow servant, as I had mercy on you?' And in anger his master delivered him to the jailers, until he should pay all his debt. So also my heavenly Father will do to every one of you, if you do not forgive your brother from your heart."

Matthew 18:23–35

The first servant was the recipient of an overwhelming mercy. His astronomical debt was forgiven. If you have repented of your sins and trusted Christ, this is you. You have received the mercy of God. You will not receive the punishment for your sins that you rightly deserve, because your debt has been paid for you through Jesus' work on the cross. However, even though the servant had received this mercy, he was unwilling to show mercy, even for a small debt, to his fellow servant. Seeing this, the king put the first servant in prison. Jesus didn't mince words when He said, "*So also my heavenly Father will do to every one of you, if you do not forgive your brother from your heart.*" We will experience divine consequences and will be in bondage if we are not people of mercy. Here are three practical ways we can seek healing in our family relationships by showing mercy.

Mercy Is Choosing Not to Bring Up Past Sins

Dan and Kate had been married just over four years, and there was more good than bad in their relationship. They were eagerly anticipating the arrival of their first child in just a few months. Even though things were generally good, the start of their relationship had been rocky. They dated on and off again through high school and college. But during one of the "on" times, Dan had a fling with another girl. Understandably, this caused a huge wound for Kate and did significant damage to their relationship. Dan genuinely repented and worked to rebuild trust. God brought them through a process of forgiveness and healing. After they graduated from college, both of their families were in support of their marriage.

It was only a few months into their marriage when a pattern began to emerge. When they would have arguments, Kate would repeatedly bring up Dan's cheating. This predictably would make the conflict worse. Let's unpack this. Dan and Kate had taken the time and intentionality to work through this major issue. Dan had come clean, taken responsibility, asked for forgiveness, and demonstrated his ongoing faithfulness. Kate had chosen to forgive him and extended new trust as he proved worthy of it. However, she was still healing from the wound. This was a big one. Yes, the wound had been cleaned out, treated, and bandaged up, but it was still healing. Therefore, when Kate experienced conflict and hurt with Dan, the pain from this wound came to the surface.

Through counseling with her pastor, the Lord revealed to Kate that while it was understandable and normal to continue to feel the pain from this event, her *choice* to continually bring up Dan's sin in the middle of their arguments was causing damage to her marriage. She was, in fact, continuing to punish him, even though she had made the choice to forgive him. She was convicted that she needed to show Dan *mercy*. Her choice began to make a big difference in their relationship. They were better able to resolve conflicts. Kate felt a greater sense of freedom and healing. In addition, when those feelings of hurt and anger arose from Dan's past sins, Kate was able to share those with him in *separate* conversations. This was healthy for Kate and also enabled Dan to be more compassionate toward Kate's healing process. Forgiveness and showing mercy, for Kate, did not mean *forgetting* what Dan did (that may not happen), but making the intentional choice not to punish him by rubbing his nose in his past sin.

Mercy Is Choosing Not to Give the Cold Shoulder

There are many ways that we continue to punish our family members for their past sins. One subtle way is through the "cold shoulder" or, more overtly, with the silent treatment. Dana and Liz were sisters. Dana was married, Liz divorced. They each had two children with summer birthdays, so those weeks were full of parties and family gatherings. One of the major areas of stress in their relationship was the result of their different parenting styles and expectations of their children's behavior. It was not uncommon for Liz's kids to play more rough and wild and for Dana's children to be upset and not wanting to play. When Dana confronted Liz about this, Liz's reaction seemed harsh and flippant, even when Dana's children had been physically hurt.

In their family system, it was not normal for these differences and conflicts to be talked through in a productive way. Instead, tempers would flare, between the children and between the moms, and one family would look for a quick way to leave the gathering. Finally, Dana's husband insisted that the parents needed to try to talk through this ongoing situation to seek healing and build some healthier patterns. The conversation went well. Apologies were offered and accepted. They agreed to be more proactive with the children and provide them with better supervision.

At the next birthday party, Dana was clearly cold and aloof. She did not greet her sister when Liz and her family arrived.

When Liz walked into a room, Dana quietly left. When Liz tried to strike up a conversation, her sister gave one-word answers. What was going on? Even though the conversation had gone well and forgiveness had been extended, Dana was still fuming and angry about the past conflicts, specifically those situations in which her kids had been hurt. She was giving Liz the cold shoulder to punish her. Dana's kids had been hurt, so this was a way to hurt her sister. Sadly, the day went from bad to worse. Imagine if Dana had made the *choice* not to punish Liz for past problems and conflicts!

In some ways, this situation worsened because of an ongoing lack of direct communication. The point here is not that you should pretend to be nice to everyone, even if you are hurting and angry. Dana had two options to bring fresh healing to her relationship with Liz. One option would have been to show *mercy*—to not punish her with the cold shoulder, but intentionally greet her, talk with her, and spend time with her at the party. The other option would have been to privately say, "Liz, I am glad we were able to talk a couple of weeks ago about the problems we were having with the kids and between us. It was good to be honest and to forgive each other. However, I need to tell you that I'm still struggling emotionally with all of this. I am asking God to help me with my anger. So if I seem a little distant today, that is why. I think things are moving in the right direction, and I'm committed to doing my part, but it's just taking time for me to heal." This would be an example of a direct-but-loving boundary, which likely would have prevented new conflicts and hurt from taking place that day.

Mercy Is Choosing Not to Take Vengeance

When we are deeply wounded by a family member, our sinful nature desires vengeance. We addressed a portion of this earlier in the book when we looked at the spiritual warfare surrounding our families. Justice is a good thing. God is a God of justice. He is holy and fair, so He brings proper punishment against sin

> When we are deeply wounded
> by a family member, our sinful
> nature desires vengeance.

and sinner. However, when it comes to meting out justice, He gives His children a careful instruction: "*Vengeance is mine, I will repay, says the Lord*" (Romans 12:19).

Tragically, Debbie was sexually molested by her thirty-year-old uncle when she was in the ninth grade. There were a few incidents. It was not until she was in college that she shared what had happened with her parents. Her parents believed her and were overwhelmed. They talked through what happened, how they could have missed it, and why Debbie had not come to them sooner. In many ways, her parents responded well. They affirmed their love for her. They gave her a safe place to share her pain, trauma, anger, and fear. They also made quick plans to help Debbie connect with an excellent Christian counselor.

However, they made a significant mistake. As they talked about how to handle this with the family, and specifically with the uncle, they decided not to say anything. They saw the uncle only a couple of times a year as it was, and they would just do their best to avoid him. They even talked about Romans 12:19, "*Vengeance is mine, I will repay.*" The parents said to Debbie, "If God has consequences for your uncle, that is His job. Let's trust Him with that." While there is a portion of truth here, and the virtue of mercy is elevated, I want to suggest that in this case the parents misapplied this Scripture.

Debbie's uncle committed a serious crime, not only against Debbie and the family but also against society. It is *unjust* for a crime like this to be ignored. In our country, the standard punishment for such a crime would be incarceration. Now, here is the key point. It is not Debbie's parents' job to go grab the uncle and lock him up in the basement. That would be taking vengeance. It *is*, however, her parents' job to call the police and report the crime. Lord willing, the police and the courts would then fulfill *their* responsibilities to prosecute and bring fair punishment. In addition, Debbie's father and other family members may have a necessary role in directly confronting the uncle.

I don't want these relatively brief comments to come across as flippant or oversimplified. In matters of abuse, the privacy of the victim is of high value and should be considered when it comes to what information is shared with extended family. As I have said earlier, the purpose of this book is not to serve as a specialized, focused resource for abuse recovery. My point here is that calling the police to report sexual abuse is *not* taking vengeance, unchristian, unloving, or mean-spirited. It is, in fact, trusting *God* to bring "repayment" and just punishment to a victimizer as He sees fit. When families report abuse to the proper authorities, as difficult as that is, it serves as a positive step toward future healing. Sweeping things under the rug, for the victim and for the family, is a step backward. Notifying the authorities is also a necessary step to stop any potential ongoing abuse that might be taking place. Finally, we can pray that God will use legal consequences in a person's life (such as imprisonment) to drive them to genuine repentance.

Mercy Can Ripple through the Generations

At multiple points in this book, we have turned our attention to the miraculous reconciliation between Joseph and his brothers.

159

Mercy played a central role in their family healing. Joseph's brothers knelt before him. They did not know his true identity. In that moment, he could have had them all imprisoned or killed. Even later, after they had shown their repentance and begged for Benjamin to be spared, Joseph could have exercised his power to punish them for what they did to him. After all, they had it coming. Justice would have been served. An eye for an eye, and a tooth for a tooth.

But Joseph chose to show mercy. He did not punish them, even though they deserved it. Consider the impact of Joseph's decision. His family was reunited, they endured the famine, and Jacob was overjoyed to be reunited with his son. But those blessings were just the beginning. God chose to put this account in His Word. It has been read and shared billions of times. Here we are, more than 3,500 years after these events, learning, growing, and being inspired because of all that God did in this family, and specifically through Joseph. Imagine how God desires to use *mercy* not only to impact your current family situation, but also to bring blessing and transformation for generations to come.

Questions for Reflection and Discussion

1. Which one of your family members is "rich in mercy"? What is it about this person, or what have they done, that causes you to say that?
2. Do you struggle with bringing up past sins in the middle of current conflicts?
3. Ask the Lord to show you a clear way you can show mercy to a family member this week. What would it look like to stop punishing them for their past failure?

Chapter 12

Healing through the Generations

For the Lord is good; his steadfast love endures forever, and his faithfulness to all generations.

Psalm 100:5

Amy and I are watching the unfolding of a miracle. Right now, God is working a *generational* miracle of healing and transformation in our family tree. I have shared with you the story of my father, who did not grow up in a Christian home. He was married four times, with my mother being his fourth wife. My mother grew up in a home where there was nominal church attendance, but she did not have a personal relationship with Jesus. My mother also was divorced before she met and married my father. When I was three months old, my parents' marriage was falling apart, and my mother was becoming increasingly depressed. She was even to the point of considering putting my older brother and me in a car and driving the three of us off a cliff together. It was in this time of brokenness that God brought a friend into my mother's life who shared with her the good news of Jesus. The grace of God worked in her life and brought her to repentance of her sins and faith in Christ, and she was born again! When I was a baby, I got a brand-new mom.

My mom began to attend church, and despite some resistance from my father, she brought my brother and me with her. She shared the gospel with us and led us both to put our faith and trust in Christ. My brother, Marc, and I were now the first two Christian men in our recent family tree! God was on the move, working a miracle of healing in the generations of our family.

While my mother was growing as a new Christian, my father thought my mom had become a "Jesus freak." He became more and more resistant to spiritual conversations. His unfaithfulness, as well as other unhealthy patterns in their marriage, led to their divorce when I was fifteen. But even the things that Satan intends for evil, God can use for good. The loss of my family drove me closer to the Lord. God used that pain to give me a heart and desire to go into youth and family

> **Even the things that Satan intends for evil, God can use for good.**

ministry. The Lord also enabled my brother and me to commit ourselves to seek lifelong Christian marriages. We believed that God was on the move and that He wanted *generational progress* in our family tree. That is exactly what God is doing!

Marc and I have each been blessed beyond measure with wives who love Jesus and who are committed to our marriages. Between us we have ten children, who at this moment are, by the grace of God, all walking with the Lord. Marc has four grandchildren, who are being shepherded and encouraged by their parents to follow Jesus. When it comes to healing family relationships, we must have a *multigenerational perspective*. Of course, we all want the short-term blessing of a healed marriage or a reconciled relationship with our sibling, but God's vision for healing is far greater—extending to the many generations yet to be born.

I once attended a parenting seminar with Chuck Stecker.[1] He said something I will never forget: "As Christian parents, our prayer is that our ceiling will be our kids' floor." I wish my "ceiling" were higher. I wish I were leaving my children with more virtue, character, and faith. I wish I were leaving them with less sin and selfishness. My prayer is that whatever good that God has brought about in my life will be passed on to my kids, and that all my sins and failures will be left in my generation and not carried into the next. I can't tell you how much I want my children to love Jesus more than I do, to trust His Word more than I do, and to carry the gospel further than I can. Amy and I would both say we want all our children to be better spouses and parents than we are. We believe it is happening, right before our eyes. We are witnessing the miracle of *generational* progress and healing, even in the middle of our daily struggles.

Multigenerational Vision in Psalm 78

Faithfulness and growth through the generations is a major theme in Scripture and is near to the heart of God. One of the most powerful visions for multigenerational faith and connection is found in Psalm 78:

> Give ear, O my people, to my teaching;
> incline your ears to the words of my mouth!

I will open my mouth in a parable;
I will utter dark sayings from of old, things that we
have heard and known,
that our fathers have told us.
We will not hide them from their children,
but tell to the coming generation
the glorious deeds of the Lord, and his might,
and the wonders that he has done.

vv. 1–4

These first four verses give a picture of the power of the family in passing faith in God down through the generations. First, there is an affirmation that what we have heard and what we know of God has come to us from our fathers, the generations before us, both within our families and within the faith community. Because we have *received* the faith generationally, we are called to *share* it generationally. In the next three verses, we see the extraordinary impact that can happen through faithful, healthy families:

He established a testimony in Jacob
and appointed a law in Israel,
which he commanded our fathers
to teach to their children,
that the next generation might know them,
the children yet unborn,
and arise and tell them to their children,
so that they should set their hope in God
and not forget the works of God,
but keep his commandments.

vv. 5–7

Here we find God's command for fathers to intentionally teach and spiritually disciple their children. Now look at the generational impact. It begins simply, "*He commanded our fathers to teach their children, that the next generation might know them*" (vv. 5–6). God wants me to have a loving, close,

---

Because we have **received** the faith generationally, we are called to **share** it generationally.

---

healthy relationship with my children, so that He can use me to help them follow Him. But it doesn't stop there. God's vision is not just that our families would lead our children to follow Him, but also that they (our children) would lead our unborn grandchildren to love Him! It is our unborn grandchildren who are being spoken of in the verse that says "*the children yet unborn*" (v. 6).

Now look at the next part of the verse, "*[that they might] arise and tell them to their children*" (v. 6). What is happening here? My unborn grandchildren are telling my unborn great-grandchildren about the great and glorious deeds of the Lord. And what is the result? "*They should set their hope in God*" (v. 7). Who is setting their hope in God? My unborn great-grandchildren! This is the gospel, kingdom, missional, and generational impact of a Christian family. A central motivation for confronting our family problems today is the ripple effect in the kingdom of God in generations to come.

Cultivating, Sowing, and Reaping

God frequently communicates spiritual truths using agricultural analogies. Earlier, we considered Hebrews 12:15, "*See to it that no one fails to obtain the grace of God; that no 'root* of bitterness' springs up and causes trouble, and by it many become defiled." Perhaps the most simple of all these pictures in Scripture is this: "Do not be deceived: God is not mocked, for whatever one sows, that will he also reap" (Galatians 6:7). "You reap what you sow" has made it from the pages of the Bible into our cultural lexicon.

When it comes to cultivating, sowing, and reaping, we like the reaping part. Harvest time! We want to enjoy the fruit. But the fruit does not come without the hard work of preparing the soil and planting the seed and the ongoing watering, care, and protection. Reaping is the end of a long, difficult process. These principles also apply to our current family relationships and to future generations.

Perhaps you are one of the first Christians in your family tree. As you look around the "garden" of your family and extended family, you see all kinds of weeds (conflicts), and the ground is more rocks (anger, distance, hardness) than soil. You feel as though your ministry in your family is nothing but pulling weeds and breaking up the rocks. Cultivating is exhausting. When will you ever get to plant some seeds? When will you finally get some fruit and see the blessings of God in your family? It is easy to become overwhelmed with hopelessness and discouragement.

If this is how you are feeling, you need *multigenerational vision*. You have to know and believe in your heart that God works to transform families through the generations. Your calling to follow Jesus is not just about you. What if God were to come to you and say, "I have called you to follow me. I have brought you from darkness to light, from death to life. I have put you in a garden full of weeds and rocks. My calling on your life is to break rocks and pull weeds. Your life will be dedicated to cultivating. Your children will then get some seeds planted, and your grandchildren will reap a harvest"? If God gave you this assignment, what would you do? I know what I would do! I would get back to work pulling weeds and breaking up rocks. My heart would be strengthened and renewed, knowing my labor was not in vain. The more we understand God's desire

> You have to know and
> believe in your heart that God
> works to transform families
> through the generations.

and power to work generationally in our families, the more faithful and courageous we will be in seeking to love our family members here and now.

Even If We Should Be But Stepping-Stones

One of the greatest examples of multigenerational vision can be found in the history of the Pilgrims. Perhaps you remember the story. In the early 1600s, a small group of Christians relocated their little church from England to Holland in order to worship God according to the Scriptures and their conscience. However, after about ten years, the economic and spiritual conditions there drove them to consider a more radical move. They set their sights on the New World and crossed the ocean in the summer of 1620.

In his book *Of Plymouth Plantation*, William Bradford recorded the firsthand account of their journey and the establishment of their church and community on a new continent. He explains in detail why this group of Christian believers was willing to risk everything, their lives and their families, in this adventure:

We cherish a great hope, and an inward zeal, of laying good foundations for the advance of the Gospel of the Kingdom of Christ to the remote parts of the earth, even if we should be but stepping-stones to others in the performance of so great a work.[2]

These words are special to me. I have taken hold of them as a mission statement for our family. My children gave me a large framed plaque with these words written on it, which hangs in my home office right now. I love this mission statement because it's centered on "the advance of the Gospel of the Kingdom of Christ." But this is a *generational* work. Lord, would you use my struggling family, here and now, to lay some good foundations? Maybe then my children and grandchildren can build on them. Lord, if you want to use my life and our family as a "stepping-stone" for future generations to stand on, so be it! Help us be faithful and obedient today, so unborn children can better live for you tomorrow.

God honored the Pilgrims' vision. Roughly half of the *Mayflower*'s passengers died during the first winter, yet in the mercy and sovereign plan of God, He used this little church to lay the foundations for a nation unlike any other in history. Churches were planted. The gospel was preached. Slaves were freed. Missionaries were sent. Humanitarian aid was given. Freedom was proclaimed. God enabled them to fulfill their mission of "laying good foundations" and serving as "stepping-stones to others." Would you allow God to use you to lay good foundations for future generations of your family? Would you be willing to simply be a stepping-stone upon which your grandchildren could stand?

Questions for Reflection and Discussion

1. How do you see God working in the generations of your family?

2. Prior to reading this chapter, how much had you thought about the principle of multigenerational vision? How would your attitude and heart toward your family problems change if you were to capture more of this vision?

3. If you are one of the first Christians in your family tree, what do you need right now to stay strong in your faith and ministry to your family?

4. Perhaps you are blessed to come from many generations of faithful Christians. How might God be calling you to accelerate your faithfulness so that this blessing can be passed on to future generations?

Chapter 13

A Family Miracle

May the God of hope fill you with all joy and peace in believing, so that by the power of the Holy Spirit you may abound in hope.

Romans 15:13

At different points in our journey together, I have shared with you about my relationship with my father. Now let me tell you the end of the story. It was June of 2008. My father, at the age of ninety, was living in Connecticut, and my family was in Illinois. We received word from my dad that he had been diagnosed with advanced cancer and likely had only months to live. When the news arrived, I was speaking at a family ministry conference in Arizona, and Amy was home with our children. She gathered the children together and helped them write cards to their grandfather. A few years before this, my father had expressly communicated to Amy that if she or the children were to send cards to him, he didn't want any Jesus stuff in there. Well, Amy thought this was a good opportunity to throw that out the window.

The children wrote four cards with crayons, markers, drawings, and Scriptures. Lissy, who was nine years old, wrote, "God loves you. We're praying for you. Heaven rocks! For God so loved the world that he sent his one and only son that whoever believes in him will not perish **but have eternal life.**" She used a fat purple marker for that last part. Our son RW, the oldest at eleven, wrote the following: "Dear Papa Bill, we are praying for you. For all have sinned and fallen short of the glory of God. I hope you enjoy this verse. Love, RW." I'm not sure that Romans 3:23 is a verse that one "enjoys," but unless you believe its truth, you cannot be saved. The four cards were completed and put in the mail.

On the tenth of August, my mother decided to visit my dad in the hospital. She was accompanied by her husband, Jack. (My mother remarried five years after my parents' divorce.) Can you picture this from my dad's perspective? Your fourth wife and her husband come to visit you in the hospital. I'm thankful that my parents were cordial toward one another postdivorce, but this must have been a bit awkward. When my mother and Jack came into his room, my father asked them, "Is there anything I can do for you?" What an odd question. He was dying. He didn't have much money. I am not sure what he was thinking. But my stepfather, Jack, answered his question, "Yes! You can trust Christ. We want to be in heaven with you."

My father paused for a moment, then replied, "I've been thinking a lot about that lately." Then, pointing to the four cards taped to his hospital room window, he said, "Bring me those cards." They read the cards together, which contained bad news, "For all have sinned and fallen short of the glory of God," and good news, "Whoever believes in him will not perish but have eternal life." This was the power of Psalm 78 in reverse. Cards from my dad's young grandchildren, packed with God's words, had impacted his heart.

My mother proceeded to share the gospel with my father. He had heard it hundreds of times before. When she finished, she asked him, "Bill, are you ready to trust Christ?"

"Yes, I am," he answered. My dad then prayed with my mom, confessed his sins, and asked Jesus to save him!

After they returned home, my mom quickly called us in Illinois to share the miraculous news. We celebrated! I had been praying for what felt like my entire life for my father's salvation. My wife and children had been praying along with me. God had answered our prayers. My mom and Jack went back the next day to see my dad. Candidly, they wanted to see if what had happened that Sunday evening was real. Perhaps he was losing his mind? Perhaps it was the medication? So my mother asked him, "Bill, do you remember praying with us yesterday?"

"Yes!" he said.

"Would it be okay if we read the Bible with you?" she asked.

"I would love that."

The miracle had indeed happened. Numerous times in my parents' marriage, my mom had suggested reading from the Bible at the dinner table. My father would have nothing to do with it. *He was a changed man.*

Reconciliation

Our family soon got in the car and made the long drive to Connecticut. I spent three incredible days with my *new* father, including a special time together on my birthday. There were so many powerful moments. He asked for my forgiveness for the things he had done to hurt the family. This was a time of true reconciliation. Back in chapter 1, we walked through the three phases of forgiveness. Phase 1 is forgiveness with the will. Phase 2 is forgiveness with the heart. Phase 3 is reconciliation.

God had brought me through the first two phases. I had made the choice to forgive my dad. God had then, over the course of many years, drained my heart of my anger and bitterness toward him. As far as I was concerned, I had forgiven him and I was now free. There was no "ball and chain" of resentment attached to my life. Our relationship for many years was pleasant and cordial. We talked about baseball and the news. We enjoyed some activities. He paid for our family to travel out to Connecticut each year so we could spend time together. But our relationship was not *reconciled*. I'll never forget my father saying to me from his hospital bed, "I am so glad we can finally talk about things that matter."

A broken relationship cannot truly reconcile until the offender asks for forgiveness from the offended. In most family conflicts, this needs to be a two-way street, as both parties have offended and been offended. We all must face this difficult reality when it comes to seeking healing in our family relationships. Reconciliation may never happen. The offender may never genuinely ask for our forgiveness. However, even if that does not happen, God desires and has the power to bring us to a place of freedom. We can be free from anger and bitterness. We can be

> **God desires and has the power to bring us to a place of freedom.**

free to be cordial and pleasant with our family members. More important, we can be free to *love* and, "as far as it depends on us," seek peace (see Romans 12:18). Through God's mercy, I had the "gift of forgiveness" prepared for my father. But a gift cannot be forced on a person. It must be desired and received. These moments of reconciliation, as you might imagine, were filled with tears.

A New Life Verse

During an afternoon visit with my dad, he announced, "Bobby, I have a new life verse." Before he came to Christ, he'd had a "life verse," but it was not from the Bible. It was from "Invictus," a famous poem by William Ernest Henley. A portion of Henley's poem was inscribed on a little plaque prominently displayed on the desk in my dad's home office:

> Beyond this place of wrath and tears
> Looms but the Horror of the shade,
> And yet the menace of the years
> Finds and shall find me unafraid.
>
> It matters not how strait the gate,
> How charged with punishments the scroll,
> I am the master of my fate,
> I am the captain of my soul.[1]

My father had led his life shaking his fist at God, rejecting both His justice and His mercy. As far as my dad was concerned, he was going to call the shots on Judgment Day. But now things had changed.

"Bobby, I have a new life verse." I laughed a little, waiting to hear what was coming next. Dad continued, "Here is my new life verse. 'There but for the grace of God, go I.'" Now, that "verse" is not found in the Bible either,[2] but I thought it was a dramatic improvement on the previous one. This is one of the Scriptures I read with my father:

> He does not deal with us according to our sins, nor repay us according to our iniquities. For as high as the heavens are above the earth, so great is his steadfast love toward those who fear him; as far as the east is from the west, so far does he remove our transgressions from us. As a father shows compassion to

his children, so the Lord shows compassion to those who fear
him. For he knows our frame; he remembers that we are dust.

Psalm 103:10–14

My father had a total reorientation of his attitude toward
God. The Lord moved him from pride and arrogance to humility and neediness. He had now experienced both sides of James
4:6 and Luke 14:11, "*God opposes the proud but gives grace
to the humble*" and "*For everyone who exalts himself will be
humbled, and he who humbles himself will be exalted.*"

The time had come for us to head back to Illinois. I knew
my dad's body would give out in a few weeks. I'll never forget
saying good-bye to him, walking out of the care center, climbing
into my car, and weeping. This would be the last time I would
see my dad in this life. But everything had changed! I looked
forward to heaven more than ever before. We only had three
days here as brothers in Christ, but the day is coming soon when
we will have new bodies and be together again on a new earth.
Bill Rienow was received by his Savior on September 3, 2008.

It's Not Too Late!

We prayed for decades for my father's salvation and for the
reconciliation of our relationship. Decades. What was God
doing? Why was He not answering? Did He not care, or was
my father too difficult a case for Him? There were many seasons of discouragement, prayerlessness, and passive resigna-
tion that things would never change. But God demonstrated to
our family the truth found in Isaiah 59:1: "*Behold, the Lord's
hand is not shortened, that it cannot save, or his ear dull, that
it cannot hear.*"

Perhaps you have a list of questions you want to ask God.
Some of mine are, "Why did you wait so long to save my dad?

Why was it the 805th time he heard the gospel that he repented? Why not the second time?" While I don't know the answers to such questions, I firmly believe God's timing is perfect. He is never slow, delayed, or behind schedule. God glorified himself

> **It is not too late for God to work a miracle in your family.**

(He made himself look good!) through His work in my father's life and in bringing generational healing to our family.

It is not too late for God to work a miracle in your family. Don't stop praying. Don't stop trusting God's power, plan, and timetable. You don't know when God will move with overwhelming and miraculous power. Many of us face crises and brokenness in our families that are humanly impossible to heal. I believe Jesus would speak to us and say, "*With man this is impossible, but with God all things are possible*" (Matthew 19:26).

Questions for Reflection and Discussion

1. Have you seen God work miracles of healing and salvation in your family tree? Consider some of those stories now. Thank God for His work in those situations and look for an opportunity to share one of those stories with a friend or family member this week.

2. If you have been in a difficult family situation for a long time, you will need support for the journey. Are there other family members who can pray with you and partner with you in seeking peace and healing? Are there Christian friends you could call to ask them to support

you in prayer or even meet with you occasionally to pray with you?

3. Are you facing a humanly hopeless situation? Look again at Matthew 19:26 written above. Do you believe Jesus' words? Take time and talk with God now, asking Him to give you renewed faith and hope for the future of your family. Ask Him to renew your passion and persistence in prayer.

Conclusion

Reconciliation with God

Therefore, if anyone is in Christ, he is a new creation. The old has passed away; behold, the new has come. All this is from God, who through Christ reconciled us to himself and gave us the ministry of reconciliation; that is, in Christ God was reconciling the world to himself, not counting their trespasses against them, and entrusting to us the message of reconciliation.

2 Corinthians 5:17–19

You have read this book because you care about your family and want to seek healing in your family. However, there is something far more important than reconciling family relationships, and that is reconciling with God. The title of this book is *Healing Family Relationships*, but that is not the end goal. In heaven, there will be no Rienow family, Smith family, or Chang family. Our temporary earthly families will gloriously come together in one eternal family. God created our earthly families to prepare us for life in our eternal family. It may be that God has allowed this painful conflict into your life to bring you to himself. If you have not experienced God's forgiveness of your sins, you will ultimately be unable to forgive others of their sins. If you have not been brought into a right relationship with God, you will be unable to be in right relationships with your family members.

Throughout the book, I have tried to point us to the goodness, grace, and mercy of God as our model for healing our families. In these final pages, if you are unsure of where you stand with God, or you are unsure of your place in God's eternal family, I want to share God's good news with you.

Bad News

But before we get to the good news, we have to start with the bad news. This will not be easy to hear, but it is true. When you and I were conceived, we were sinners. When our first parent, Adam, sinned, the entire human race was infected. Actually, *infected* is too soft. When Adam sinned, we all died, spiritually speaking. You can cure an infection. You can't cure death. God explains this bleak reality to us this way:

> And you were dead in the trespasses and sins in which you once walked, following the course of this world, following the prince of the power of the air, the spirit that is now at work in the sons of disobedience—among whom we all once lived in the passions of our flesh, carrying out the desires of the body and the mind, and were by nature children of wrath, like the rest of mankind.
>
> Ephesians 2:1–3

God describes us in three ways. First, He says we come into this world "*dead in trespasses and sins.*" Second, He tells us we naturally follow "*the prince of the power of the air,*" referring to the devil. Third, He rightly confronts us about our sinful behavior as we carry out "*the passions of our flesh.*" The bad news is that we are dead, devilish, and disobedient. There is nothing we can do to get rid of our sins or clean ourselves up. No amount of "good deeds" can tip the scale in our favor against our sins. In fact, it only takes one sin to disqualify us from heaven. Consider these words from Psalm 24:

> Who shall ascend the hill of the Lord? And who shall stand in his holy place? He who has clean hands and a pure heart, who does not lift up his soul to what is false and does not swear deceitfully.
>
> vv. 3–4

Who is qualified for heaven? Who is good enough to "get in"? Who will God accept? Only a perfect person, one who has clean hands and a pure heart. That leaves you and me out in the cold.

Unfortunately, the bad news is about to get worse. Because of our dead and sinful nature and behavior, we are subject to the wrath of God. God is totally fair and just. Sin and sinners are given the fair and righteous punishment. What is that? God says, *"The wages of sin is death"* (Romans 6:23). The fair penalty for our rebellion against God is death—spiritual death, physical death, and eternal separation from Him.

People respond to these realities in one of two ways. Some say, "If that is who God is and what Christianity is all about, then I want nothing to do with it." But others say, "If I am dead in my sin and deserve God's wrath, what must I do to be saved?" If *that* is your response, there is good news!

Good News

There is nothing we can do to save ourselves, but God has done something amazing to save us, forgive us, and bring us into a love relationship with Him. John 3:16 may be the most famous verse in the Bible, and for good reason. The good news of God's love is captured here. *"For God so loved the world, that he gave his only Son, that whoever believes in him should not perish but have eternal life."* Despite your sin, God loves you, and He proved it. *"But God shows his love for us in that while we were still sinners, Christ died for us"* (Romans 5:8). God became a man in His Son, Jesus. He lived a perfect life. Then your sins and my sins were put on Him, and when He died on the cross, He paid the death penalty on our behalf. In this way, God's holy justice was satisfied, your sin was rightly punished, and a path to forgiveness was created. Seven hundred years before Jesus died on the cross, God spoke through the prophet Isaiah:

> But he was pierced for our transgressions; he was crushed for our iniquities; upon him was the chastisement that brought us peace, and with his wounds we are healed. All we like sheep have gone astray; we have turned—every one—to his own way; and the Lord has laid on him the iniquity of us all.
>
> Isaiah 53:5–6

Jesus died on a Friday afternoon. But that was not the end. On Sunday morning, He was resurrected—conquering sin, death, and the devil. Anyone can die. Only Jesus has conquered death, demonstrating He was not just a prophet or moral teacher, but God's one and only Son. He is alive today in heaven and is coming back again. Jesus said, *"I am the resurrection and the life. Whoever believes in me, though he die, yet shall he live"* (John 11:25).

Respond Today

Are you at peace with God? Have you received forgiveness for your sins? God's love and Christ's work have done all that is necessary. Jesus now calls you to *respond* with repentance and faith. This was the call of Christ in His first sermon recorded in the book of Mark. *"The time is fulfilled, and the kingdom of God is at hand; repent and believe in the gospel"* (Mark 1:15). Repentance and faith can go together in one honest prayer: "God, I confess that I am a sinner in need of a savior. I believe that Jesus took my sins, died in my place, and rose again from the dead. I am putting my faith in Jesus to save me and change me."

You might ask, "Is that it? I say a little prayer and I am for-given, saved from hell, and promised heaven?" No, it's not the little prayer, as if it were a series of magic words that come out of your mouth. But if words like these are a genuine overflow of your repentant heart before God and an expression of your choice to trust Jesus rather than yourself, then yes, this "little prayer" will change everything, now and forever. Consider this promise from God:

> If you confess with your mouth that Jesus is Lord and believe in your heart that God raised him from the dead, you will be saved. For with the heart one believes and is justified, and with the mouth one confesses and is saved. For the Scripture says, "Everyone who believes in him will not be put to shame." For there is no distinction between Jew and Greek; for the same Lord is Lord of all, bestowing his riches on all who call on him. For "everyone who calls on the name of the Lord will be saved."
>
> Romans 10:9–13

Every other religion of the world will offer you a list of the good deeds you need to do to "make it to the good place." Christianity alone says that there is nothing you can do to earn forgiveness and salvation, but instead it has been earned for you by God's Son. It can only be received by faith. It may be that the Holy Spirit of God is right now working in your heart, filling you with a spirit of repentance for your sins and faith in Christ! Respond to God right now in prayer.

Many people over the years have told me that they will figure out "the God stuff" later. They were too busy at the moment to worry about "religious things." Here is the problem with that way of thinking. You don't know how much more time you have. *"It is appointed for man to die once, and after that comes judgment"* (Hebrews 9:27). If you haven't yet entered into the family of God through Jesus, don't wait another hour. Repent. Believe. Be saved.

Healing Family Relationships

God desires that you be reconciled to Him and reconciled with your family. He wants you to be at peace with Him and at peace with your family. As we grow in our faith and relationship with Jesus, we can then, through His power and strength, choose attitudes and actions that lead to peace in our families. Many times, all through the New Testament, we see God work a miracle of grace in the life of an individual that then spreads to their entire household!

> "And he told us how he had seen the angel stand in his house and say, 'Send to Joppa and bring Simon who is called Peter; he will declare to you a message by which you will be saved, you and all your household.'"
>
> Acts 11:13–14

> One who heard us was a woman named Lydia, from the city of Thyatira, a seller of purple goods, who was a worshiper of God. The Lord opened her heart to pay attention to what was said by Paul. And after she was baptized, and her household

as well, she urged us, saying, "If you have judged me to be faithful to the Lord, come to my house and stay." And she prevailed upon us.

Acts 16:14–15

Then he brought them out and said, "Sirs, what must I do to be saved?" And they said, "Believe in the Lord Jesus, and you will be saved, you and your household." And they spoke the word of the Lord to him and to all who were in his house. And he took them the same hour of the night and washed their wounds; and he was baptized at once, he and all his family. Then he brought them up into his house and set food before them. And he rejoiced along with his entire household that he had believed in God.

Acts 16:30–34

Take Action

The biblical principles in this book are principles of action, not ideas. My purpose has not primarily been to educate or transfer information to you, but to encourage you to step out in faith and *act* on God's call to seek healing for your family. You can't control what your family members will think, say, or do. But you can pursue healing and unity as far as it depends on you. Here are the action principles from the Bible that we have explored together. Where would God have you begin?

- Healing through prayer
- Healing through repentance
- Healing through listening
- Healing through acceptance
- Healing through spiritual warfare

- Healing through boundaries
- Healing through compassion
- Healing through patience
- Healing through mediators
- Healing through mercy
- Healing through the generations

Receive these Scriptures as blessings as you accelerate your ministry to your family.

May the God of hope fill you with all joy and peace in believing, so that by the power of the Holy Spirit you may abound in hope.

Romans 15:13

All this is from God, who through Christ reconciled us to himself and gave us the ministry of reconciliation.

2 Corinthians 5:18

God is able to make all grace abound to you, so that having all sufficiency in all things at all times, you may abound in every good work.

2 Corinthians 9:8

Questions for Reflection and Discussion

1. Have you responded to the grace of God by repenting of your sins and putting your faith in Christ? If so, tell God how thankful you are for His grace in saving you. If you are reading this book with friends, share the story of God's work of salvation in your life.

2. How does being reconciled with God through Christ, and being a part of His spiritual family, affect your life in your earthly family?

3. Is God calling you to seek healing with a specific family member? As you consider all the healing principles we have explored, what is one step you are willing to take right now?

Notes

Introduction: Every Family Is Hurting

1. Stories are shared with permission, and names have been changed to respect privacy.

Chapter 1: The Power of Forgiveness

1. Author's paraphrase of a line from *Diary of a Wimpy Kid: The Long Haul*, produced by Nina Jacobson and Brad Simpson, directed by David Bowers (United States: Twentieth Century Fox, 2017), motion picture.

2. "Falcataria moluccana," Useful Tropical Plants Database, Ken Fern, accessed December 13, 2019, http://tropical.theferns.info/viewtropical.php ?id=Falcataria+moluccana.

3. Jerry Root, student forum (Wheaton College, Wheaton IL, November 1990).

Chapter 3: Healing through Repentance

1. Emerson Eggerichs, Love and Respect Conference (Wheaton, IL, October 2018).

Chapter 4: Healing through Listening

1. The sections on avoiding blaming statements and on being comfortable with disagreement are informed by Milan and Kay Yerkovich's book *How We Love: Discover Your Love Style, Enhance Your Marriage* (New York: Crown Publishing Group, 2017), 284–296.

Chapter 6: Healing through Spiritual Warfare

1. In some situations, seeking healing in a family requires putting up relational boundaries in a toxic relationship. We will explore these situations in the next chapter.

Chapter 7: Healing through Boundaries

1. This chapter is a brief introduction to the power and importance of boundaries. If this chapter is thought provoking for you, you may want to do further reading on the topic. Consider beginning with *Boundaries: When to Say Yes, How to Say No to Take Control of Your Life* by Henry Cloud and John Townsend.

2. Rob Rienow, *Limited Church: Unlimited Kingdom: Uniting Church and Family in the Great Commission* (Nashville: Randall House Publications, 2013), 170.

3. Billy Graham, *Just As I Am: Autobiography of Billy Graham* (HarperCollins Publishers, 1997) 702, 723–724.

4. For a detailed development of how God created the family and the church to partner together in the Great Commission, I encourage you to read my book *Limited Church: Unlimited Kingdom* (Randall House Publications, 2013).

Chapter 9: Healing through Patience

1. Another area where I see Christians judging God based on the middle of the story is that of "fallen" Christian leaders. When a pastor or a "public" Christian loses their ministry due to sinful behavior, it is right for them to receive the fair consequences for their actions, both within the church and, as needed, from the criminal justice system. However, we should pray and hope that their "fall" is not the end of the story. King David had a pretty awful middle of his story. Paul's days as a Pharisee were not pretty. When fellow believers fall, we can be glad that justice is served and churches are protected, but let's also pray for God's healing and redemption.

2. I was impacted by the book *Letters from Dad: How to Leave a Legacy of Faith, Hope, and Love for Your Family* by Greg Vaughn (Nashville: Thomas Nelson, 2005). He asks a powerful question on the book's cover, "If God were to take you home today, what would your wife and children hold in their hands tomorrow that would let them know that they were the treasures of your life?"

3. Dennis Rainey, *Stepping Up: A Call to Courageous Manhood* (FamilyLife, 2011), 67–68.

Chapter 10: Healing through Mediators

1. It would be fair to interpret Jesus' instructions as applying to our relationships with other believers, which would mean our relationships at church

as well as with family members who are Christians. However, Jesus' action plan here, particularly the first two steps of private confrontation and engaging mediators, can be helpful and appropriate for all our family relationships, even if the family member with whom we are in conflict is not a follower of Jesus.

Chapter 11: Healing through Mercy

1. "3414. mna," HELPS Word-studies, Bible Hub, accessed December 17, 2019, https://biblehub.com/greek/3414.htm.

2. "5007. talanton," HELPS Word-studies, Bible Hub, accessed December 17, 2019, https://biblehub.com/greek/5007.htm.

Chapter 12: Healing through the Generations

1. Chuck Stecker, Iron Sharpens Iron (seminar, Indianapolis, IN, September 2010). For more information, go to http://chuckstecker.com.

2. William Bradford and Harold Paget, *Of Plymouth Plantation: Bradford's History of the Plymouth Settlement*, 1608–1650 (Vision Forum, 2002), 21.

Chapter 13: A Family Miracle

1. William Ernest Henley, *A Book of Verses*, 3rd ed. (New York: Scribner and Welford, 1891), 56–57.

2. My father's new "life verse" is a paraphrase of similar quotes from a number of Christians following the Reformation. See "There But For the Grace of God, Go I," *Quote Investigator* (blog), July 6, 2014, https://quote investigator.com/2014/07/06/grace/.

About the Author

Rob Rienow (DMin, Gordon-Conwell) sees his most important ministry as loving his wife, Amy, and partnering with her to help their seven children follow God. In 2011, Rob and Amy launched Visionary Family Ministries, their mission to build the church through a global reformation of family discipleship. Through their conferences, seminars, and resources they seek to equip and encourage parents, couples, families, and church leaders around the world. Rob has served as a pastor and church planter and speaks at national and international conferences, including D6, as well as on national radio. He and Amy have written several books on family relationships, including *Visionary Parenting* and *Visionary Marriage*. When Rob is not fishing for men, he enjoys fishing for fish. The Rienow family lives in a western suburb of Chicago. Learn more at www .VisionaryFam.com.

Learn More about Visionary Family Ministries

Amy and I serve as the cofounders of Visionary Family Ministries. We want to help your family grow in faith together. We encourage you to visit our website at www.VisionaryFam.com, where you will find:

- Additional Scripture-filled books, including *Visionary Parenting* and *Visionary Marriage*
- Video Bible studies for your church or small group
- Free podcast episodes of our seminars and conferences
- Blog posts to encourage your faith and family relationships
- Information about the next VFM event coming to your area, as well as information about how your church can host an event for your community

You can also connect with us personally on social media:

- Facebook: www.facebook.com/VisionaryFam
- Twitter: @VisionaryFam
- YouTube: Visionary Family Ministries
- Instagram: @VisionaryFamilyMinistries
- LinkedIn: www.linkedin.com/company/ visionary-family-ministries

With God's love,
Rob and Amy Rienow